QUILT OF SOULS

QUILT OF SOULS

Phyllis Lawson

DEDICATION PAGE

This book is dedicated to my grandmother, Lula Young Horn

My mother Evelyn Horn because without her there would be no me

My precious granddaughters who are the light of my life
My greatest wish is to provide you with the same inspiration that your
Great-great-grandmother provided me

Lula Young Horn 1883-1986

<u>My Brother</u>

Rufus Biffle Jr.
(1947- 1998)

Unrecognized talent gone too soon
So much pain and sorrow of an unfulfilled life and
Unrequited joy and happiness
You will always be the greatest poet that never knew who he was

Acknowledgements

I want to personally thank the following people for their contributions, support, inspiration, knowledge and help in creating this book.
Thank you, God, for seeing me through the times when I became so
tired, I thought I just couldn't go on. It was your strength that kept me
afloat. My husband Larry, you were the one at the finish line cheering
me on, and jumping up and down when I told you, "*it is done.*" Thank
you my loving husband. You are my rock and I love you with all my
heart. To Jan, you have been with me since day one with your unwavering encouragement and emotional support. Over thirty years ago, you
recognized my grandmother's accomplishments and her impact on my
life. From then on, you badgered me to write this book and get it done!
Your voice on the other end of the phone was my saving grace. I love
you, dear friend. To my son Lafayette, I love you and thank you for your
support and telling me to "go Mommy, go!" I always looked forward to
waking up in the morning to see your text messages of encouragement.
I will never be able to find the right words to express the deep well of
gratitude I have for you. Yaftahe, my oldest son you are a bright light
in my universe. I am so proud that you are my son. I will always love
and care for you beyond words. To Leslie Caplan, my editor, you are
one of a kind! You took the few stanzas in my song and made it into a
two hundred-piece symphony. I could have never made this book hum

without your precise, meticulous and superior editing skills. You were relentless in your determination to make this book a success. To Linda Farrow, when I needed a proofreader with an eagle eye, you were there to answer the call. I can't thank you enough. Debra, my dear friend of thirty-five years, thank you for your support and readership. A Million thanks to you Dawn for motivating me and creating an awesome outline for the book. You always told me that I had a great story to tell and to "just write woman write." A debt of gratitude to my parents and sisters and brothers, Chris, Gail, Eugene, Robert, Roy and crazy cousin Larry, who is like a brother to me in every way possible. Thank you Alison, you are a very special young lady who has provided support in a way that you just wouldn't understand. My niece and nephew, Deshaun and Dione, your feedback was invaluable. Thank you Marie for being a great reader and for always being positive when my manuscript was in its early infancy. You are awesome. To my *Writer's Group* members, I applaud you for those Sunday motivation emails. Words can't convey the inspiration and suggestions that you provided for Quilt of Souls. Each and every one of you mentioned here is an intricate part of the weave. Like the quilts Grandma used to make. Without one piece of cloth, there would be no whole.

TELL ME AND I FORGET
TEACH ME AND I REMEMBER
INVOLVE ME AND I LEARN

BEN FRANKLIN

PREFACE

There were some deep and troubled times during the 1940s and 50s when many Blacks made the long trek north to large American cities in search of better living conditions. Once they got established and began having babies, hardships arose. They'd end up sending a child or two down south to live with grandparents; grandparents they might never had met before. Just like that, a young'un would be plucked off their front porch, out of the only family they knew and without explanation, left on the doorstep of virtual strangers. Sometimes these children didn't return north until they were teenagers. Sometimes they never returned.

I was one of these "Grandma's other babies;" four years old taken from my home and driven sixteen hours down the road in a car full of strangers, to a house in the middle of nowhere, with grandparents I never met before. I was abandoned. No way around it. The stigma of being given away followed me around for many years, like a lost puppy nipping at my heels.

It took my grandmother's love and an old, tattered quilt to repair my self-esteem and return me to wholeness. She was responsible for preparing me to overcome a myriad of obstacles, and tilled the soil for my resiliency. She built me a solid foundation as I prepared to face an uncertain and harsh future over the next twenty years.

Grandma Lula told me stories of the amazing, and often tragic lives of her loved ones as she wove pieces of their clothing into quilts she made by hand. I sat and listened intensely. I connected with those people whose stories and souls were transformed into a patchwork of healing with every pull of the thread. I knew one day I'd retell them as Grandma Lula conveyed them to me.

I may have long since forgotten the first time I rode a bike, received my first kiss, or got my driver's license, but I never forgot Grandma's stories of the Quilt of Souls. They stitched my broken heart back together and healed my life.

Those heroic grandmothers of the 1950s and 60s have been passed over by history. No notice has been taken of how they toiled to raise grandchildren who were left on their doorsteps: the endless hours of changing diapers and drying the tears of those young children who were considered surplus. Like other grandmothers from her era, Grandma Lula was a pioneer, a symbol of hope who found alternative ways to soften the horrors of racism and bigotry. She made beautiful quilts as a way for people to refocus their gaze from the ugliness. Even if only temporarily.

She was an impenetrable wall that weathered all the storms of life. Through her, I learned the meaning of unconditional love. She was my rock. She taught me everything I needed to know about life, including all its twists and turns. She solidified my ability to conquer any roadblock that stood before me. I can't stop thinking about the stories of those people whose clothes were embedded into her quilts. Their lives interrupted, cut short, and the children who suffered and died needlessly.

I know these stories are what carried me through the most difficult periods of my life. The days of quilting with Grandma became a period of transformation for me. The pillars of our culture are those unwavering grandmothers who held up, and continue to hold up, multitudes of children and families. The debt of gratitude we owe these women who loved us so completely is one that can never be repaid. I honor them by embodying the lessons they taught me.

CHAPTER 1

City Girl Gone Country

M emory can be a strange thing. Sometimes you'd much rather forget because of the heartbreak attached to it. I remember climbing into the backseat of an automobile with two large men, one on each side of me. There were three towering women in the front seat; one of them had a mountain of gray hair that sat on the top of her head like a giant bush. The driver had teeth protruding from her mouth even when her lips were closed. In reality, these people could have all been midgets, but to a young, scared four- year- old, they appeared larger than life. They were piled into the vehicle like canned sardines. I don't recall anyone ever getting out of the car. They just sat there smiling as the lady in the front seat made small talk with my sister. As we drove away, I waved to my sister and brothers who pulled themselves away from their game, looking as puzzled as I was.

I didn't utter a word; never asked where I was going, or why. I didn't inquire about who these strangers were. All I knew was they surrounded me on that sixteen-hour drive on one of the hottest spring days of my life. As we passed through the countryside, I saw every four-legged animal known to man: big cows, and bigger horses; everything was bigger than me. I was a small, lost child swirling in a world of bigness.

It felt as though only moments before I sat on an old milk crate while my older sister braided my hair. She popped me upside the head with the end of the comb because I was fighting her as she wrestled with the tangles in my hair. The awful pink ribbons kept falling in my face as she attempted to tie them into neat little bows. I hated girlie ribbons. All I wanted to do was join my brothers crouched on the side-walk playing a game of marbles called "knuckles". I'd never forget the deafening sound of the ominous black car that drowned out the noise of my brothers cackling as they played. I could smell the stale stank from old engine oil that emitted out its rear end as the fumes rose up the steps and through the front screen door.

I wrenched myself away from the claws of my sister right before she placed the last ribbon on the final braid. It hung there dangling out of place. As I stared through the screen door, I didn't realize this would be the last time I'd be anywhere near my sister for a long time.

Many of the events that day remain obscured, as though a dark storm welled up and thundered out all the memories. I don't remember the exact moment when I began to miss my family, or recognize I was on my way to some unknown place, far away from them. Children weren't allowed to question grown-ups. Children were to be seen, not heard.

There were no goodbyes, no hugs, no tears and no parents. My siblings and I had always addressed my parents as Mother and Father. I often wondered how this formal title came about, especially since my parents were simple working class folks from the inner city of Detroit. Since this was the way our four older siblings referred to our parents, it trickled down to my twin brother, my two younger brothers, and me.

Obviously my parents existed, but deep in the recesses of my mind, they were a mirage to me. My sister was the only person I equated with being the 'mother figure' in my house, even though I knew our mother was around somewhere. Father worked eighteen hours a day while

Mother worked at night and slept all day long. Maybe Mother was fast asleep when the big people came and whisked me from my home. Maybe she couldn't face that she had to send me away for a long time.

During my years in the country, I struggled to remember my parents' faces. I only recall the hushed voice of Father who barely spoke at all, while Mother spoke in a loud boisterous tone that neighbors down the block could probably hear. Sometimes I'd conjure up slivers of events that occurred before I left Detroit, short snippets of my sisters and brothers. It didn't take long before their faces, too, disappeared from my memory. Childhood trauma had a way of erasing the important things.

It was only my sister who stood there as the car drove away carrying me with it. The comb still in her hand as the pink ribbon dangled back and forth from my forehead, irritating my eyelid every time I moved. I was afraid to speak or cry. I was too petrified to ask for a drink of water or go to the bathroom. That was the first time in my young life where fear stared me right in the face.

My constant shiver chattered my teeth as a bitter cold consumed my body. I could barely breathe sitting between two men whose big behinds took up every inch of available space. If they moved a fraction in either direction, they'd be sitting on my lap. I was a small child with no concept of time and space, or what it felt like to be away from the only people I knew. I'd never been this far from home. With each bump in the road, I couldn't help but wonder where that road would lead, and what was waiting for me at the end of it. I closed my eyes and tried to imagine something familiar that would ease the pain of my cavernous loss.

As the engine churned and hummed its way down the long concrete highway, I sank into the black night. I balled up in the small space I'd carved out and reeled myself into a sleep so deep, I didn't realize we'd stopped by the side of the road. Most hotels along the interstate refused to allow Black folks to use their facilities. The only way possible to rest up from a long, overnight trip was to pull over and "make do," as I heard the lady in the front seat announce to the riders.

The only emotions I knew were pain, sadness and happiness. Every other feeling was irrelevant. Security and comfort fit under the happiness umbrella, and pain and sadness fit like a glove with abandonment. What I perceived as fear could have very well been plain old suffering. My insides longed for an explanation as to why I was torn away from my family. The silence from those who knew the answers pounded inside my head. I knew the strict rules of how a child "stays in a child's place." I was not about to cross those boundaries by any means.

In the late evenings when adult friends or relatives would knock on our door, my siblings and I knew the routine: "Good Evening," yes or no ma'am or sir, then off to the basement where we remained until we'd no longer hear the chatter of their voices. This usually meant it was safe to go upstairs.

The car weaved its way past the tin-roofed homes that sat along dirt roads. Trees of every shape, size and color lined the way. As I sat on my knees peering out the back window at the trail of white dust that rose up behind us, I knew I was entering a new territory. The finality struck me like a lightning bolt as I watched the road disappear. My stomach tightened and tears were ready to bust through like a wicked storm, but in that moment, we stopped in front of a house that looked like all the other ones. A chill shook my body and my hands and feet turned ice cold. Even though the blazing Alabama sun scorched the side of my face, I shivered like I was standing dead center in a snowstorm.

I tumbled my three-foot frame from that big car while my feet searched for the ground. I landed in a bed of warm, feathery-white sand that I sank into up to my ankles. I was so caught up from the warmth of the sand as it settled around my feet I barely heard one of the men say "This is your grandpa Edgar and Madea Lula's house." The only thing that separated the car from the house was a dirt road and wire fence attached to four wooden posts that stretched the length of the front yard. A wooden gate kept the barbed wire from falling to the ground. I watched as an elderly man got up from his seat and made his way to where we stood. He was old and worn out. His khaki pants were held high above his waist with suspenders. I'd never in my life seen anyone move that slow.

I overheard the lady driver say, "Uncle Edgar is hard of hearin'." I guess that's why every time someone said, "Hey there, Uncle Edgar," he'd put one hand up to his ear and smile, not hearing a word they said. The gate swung open and the men shook hands with Grandpa Edgar as the ladies waited their turn to give him a quick hug. He looked at me and never uttered a word. He just shook his head and smiled.

Being deathly afraid made everything stand still. Even though people were moving around laughing and talking, everything warped into slow motion. My eyes darted back and forth from the big people who took me on that long ride to the old man they called Uncle Edgar. Suddenly, this smiling lady emerged from the back yard, wiping her hands on a flowery apron draped around her like a dress. "Madea Lula, how you doin'?" "Kickin', but not too high," she said as she looked down at me for the first time. "Who's this li'l skinny chile? I'm your grandma Lula, baby. You gone stay here with Grandma for a while and we gone be jus' fine."

The first thing I noted about Grandma was that she was tall and lanky, another big person in my world. Her skin was like Hershey chocolate, which was my favorite candy in the entire world. Her steel gray hair was pulled up into a tight knot on the back of her head. She had piercing grayish-blue eyes that mesmerized me with a feeling of unbidden joy. Even though this was the first time I'd ever laid eyes on her, I felt safe in her presence. The fear of the unknown overtaking every ounce of my four- year- old body dissipated while I stood there enraptured by how she glowed. Her silver hair matched the color of her eyes and her chocolate skin looked like it'd been carefully poured into a cast, molded and smoothed into a mahogany sculpture. I held tightly to one of those big people while staring at Grandma Lula, thinking about my favorite candy bar as I stood there stuck somewhere between Detroit and Livingston, Alabama.

With one swoop, Grandma Lula hugged me up so tightly, I felt like her arms were exactly where I belonged. No one in my home had ever expressed that kind of affection. No hugs, no kisses. I felt a sense of warmth from Grandma Lula's embrace and I wanted more. This beautiful, creamy cocoa skinned woman set me down, grabbed my hand and graced me with a lasting impression. She filled my senses with the distinct aroma that alternated between chocolate and mothballs.

My fascination was disrupted by the sounds of little farm animals running around. I'd never seen the likes of those creatures in all my life. They were feathery things, scurrying about in the front yard in all different colors and sizes. Some had black and white polka dots with globs of red skin hanging from their tiny little beaks. I was scared of those two-legged, slew-footed things that looked like huge birds. I found out they were chickens and roosters, and the polka dotted ones were guinea chickens. I clung to Grandma's hand tight because I was scared, but it seemed they were just as scared of me, because each time I moved, they scurried away frenzied. Grandma shooed them by flapping her apron and they scattered in fifty different directions, leaving little balls of chicken droppings as they ran away.

Grandma ushered all the big people to the front yard to "res' a spell." She dashed back and forth delivering ice-cold tea to her guests. One of the big men from the car picked up his mason jar of ice tea and gulped it down in one swoop. He let out a big "ahhhhhhh" like he'd just quenched his thirst after crossing the desert. As the big people talked and laughed, Grandma said, "Ya'll look mighty hongry so I'm gone fry up that pool of bass Edgar jus' catch this mornin'."

Grandma cooked up a feast of food in record time. When she called out, "Come on in, ya'll," I thought I'd be trampled by everyone rushing in to get up the steps and through the front door. I followed behind down a long hallway in the middle of the house and into the kitchen where the table was steaming with fresh bass from Grandpa Edgar's pond. There was fried chicken, sweet potatoes, peas, and tons of dishes I'd never seen before. The house filled up with aromas that took on a life of their own. It made my mouth water. There was food for a multitude. Grandpa Edgar sat down at the head of the table while the others sat down noisily. I climbed into a chair with my feet dangling way above the ground.

As Grandpa said grace, I sneaked a peek at the heads bowed in prayer. By the looks on their faces, you could tell they were thinking only about their hungry bellies. When the "Amen" finally came, hands from all directions reached out across the table pulling fried chicken from the serving platter and filling glasses with ice tea while gravy overflowed onto the white tablecloth. No one said a word until all the plates were loaded and everyone's mouth was full. The woman with the big teeth asked Grandpa, "So Edgar, what's that nosy sister of yours up to?" "You must be talkin' 'bout that meddlin' Bessie," answered Grandpa with a crooked grin. They laughed and began talking loudly about relatives, the weather, and how good the food was. People on both sides of me kept filling up my plate but I was too overwhelmed to eat. Grandma Lula hovered around the table, refilling glasses and urging everybody to take second helpings. She was making sure everyone was well taken care of. I longed for her to sit down and be still so I could study her chocolate face and steel gray hair, but she never did.

The big people looked even larger after digesting Grandma's food. They sat around the table burping, giggling, small talking, and chewing on toothpicks. One of the men who was in the backseat with me proclaimed how much he "hate to eat an' run," but he didn't want to be caught down there in the backwoods after dark, so "we gone ease on up the road." They filed out of the yard as if it was the end of church service, each one pausing to give Grandma, Grandpa and me a hug before they jumped in the car and took off down that long, dirt road past the oak and pine trees.

I had a gaping hole inside of me. I didn't even know these folks names, but there I sat, alone in this hot place, full of sand and trees, and God only knows what else. I sat with my legs bent and my head buried between them, smothering my heartbreak. All I wanted was to remain in darkness, until the presence of someone broke into that small space I'd created for myself. "Whatcha name, gal?" Grandpa's question knocked me out of my zone and caused my tears to erupt from my insides out. My mouth was filled with salt and sweat. Those tears had been pent up for so long, they poured out of me like a faucet. Grandpa just stared. Maybe he'd never seen tears come out of anyone like that. Grandma shook her head, came over and gathered me up into her all-consuming arms.

The day didn't improve after that. There was no running water and no inside toilets or bathtubs. No toilet paper, electricity, telephone, and absolutely no radio or television. All 'food stuff' was grown or made. Sugar, syrup and flour were from the ground, otherwise known as not "store bought," but "raised." Grandma took me to the homemade well in the back yard, which accounted for all of our drinking and bathing water. When it rained, water flowed into the gutters that lined the roof and were attached to the well. Screens covered the top to keep out leaves and bird droppings.

Then she showed me the outhouse. Bugs, wasps and every other flying insect on the planet appeared to take up permanent residence in that place. There was newspaper piled up to the ceiling which I thought was for reading. Grandma took a page from the stack and demonstrated how to rub the paper between my hands to soften it up. She wanted to make sure I did it correctly. "If you don' get that papers sof', you gonna get yo'self a case of the piles. You got to be careful with that newspaper, chile." It horrified me to think how many people down in the country might be walking around with the days headlines attached to the inside of their butts.

I held onto Grandma's hand so tightly she must have felt it all the way to her toes. Each time she explained the layout of the farm, my lips trembled like the rudders of an airplane ready to take flight. Since my two front teeth were missing, I kept my tongue firmly planted in the hole. That seemed to stop my teeth from chattering. I was a scared little girl in the middle of a huge swath of unknown.

In Detroit, I was used to everything being compact; you could walk right out the front door and the rest of the world was right there in front of you. Neighbors were a stones- throw away, and animals were non-existent. I remember my brother bringing home a stray cat. Mother was livid. She beat my brother and the cat. My brother sat for hours on the front porch with white tear tracks dried on his face. Even watching my brother being tossed out of the house by Mother for his bad decision-making, I still felt a sense of security. It was my home and it was all I knew.

Everything in my new environment frightened me. The animals had their own personal habitat, so not only did I have to adapt to my new surroundings, but I also had to adjust to theirs. The chickens terrorized me. I wept constantly and clung to Grandma for dear life. I was her shadow; when she moved, I moved.

Grandma led me through the back yard, beyond the smell and noise of the chickens and the barbed wire fence, to a huge pasture with a herd of brown, polka dot and black cows. They came running towards me, chewing on their tongues, or as Grandma called it, "chewin' on their cud." In her old southern drawl, she assured me that, "Chile, them cows more scared of you than you of them."

We walked over to the barn as I clung to her side dodging cow pies. She grabbed a rusty pail that hung on the side of the barn, pulled up a stool, and plunked it down next to one of the cows. I timidly stood behind her, but she told me to get up close so I could see. I edged in; the smell from the cow's butt made me want to puke. Each time her tail swished from left to right, the smell shot straight up my noise and down my throat. As Grandma watched me gag, she shook her head and promised that "the smell gone grow on you, chile." It smelled twice as bad as the outhouse that Grandma showed me earlier; I felt like I'd eaten a cow pie.

She wrapped her hands around the udders and began pulling. Grandma's hands were like a machine. I could tell she'd been milking for a long time. The eye contact between her and the cow astounded me. The cow was chewing on the mess in her mouth while Grandma sucked on a mouth full of snuff. They were different species, but they were in harmony with each other.

"See that? Now you try it." It took every bit of my courage, but I sat myself down on that stool. I didn't know whether I was more afraid of her tits or that long ass tail of hers that must've weighed fifty pounds. I stuck my hands under there and tried to wrap them around the cow's udders, but my fingers couldn't reach all the way. I managed to get some sort of grip and got my yanking somewhat coordinated. Brownie the cow wasn't enjoying herself as much as when Grandma was at the helm.

Her chewing suddenly stopped and her eyes evaded mine. She let out a long, painstaking "moo," which made me drop her udder right out of my hand. Grandma kept telling me to "go on gal, ol' Brownie jus' full of milk." If she had as much milk in her as I had tears flowing into that bucket, there'd be enough milk to feed the entire town of Livingston.

"Gone now, squeeze and pull, squeeze and pull, ol' Brownie waitin' on you, you hear me?" When I saw milk come squirting out, I couldn't believe it. Grandma laughed. "Why, I do declare! You a country gal now!" I didn't know whether to take my new found country gal status as a compliment or an insult. Grandma seemed a whole lot happier than me about the results. She was so proud of my milking ability that she went and found Grandpa Edgar to tell him.

Since there was no electricity and night was closing in, my grandparents prepared for darkness well before the first stars appeared. Otherwise, we'd stumble over each other in the dark. The preparation included gathering and filling kerosene lanterns. On that particular spring night, it was unusually cold. The chill possessing my body was likely the product of my uncertainty of what my first night in the country would bring. Grandpa felt sorry for me as I stood in the half lit room shaking like a leaf.

"Don' stand thar watchin' me gal, g'wine git in dat bed while I start dis here fire." Grandpa had a pile of wood stacked neatly next to the fireplace. I got into my bed, which was in Grandma and Grandpa's room. There were two large beds made of duck and goose feathers so high off the floor that I had a difficult time launching myself up there.

I shivered to the bone despite the heat from the roaring fire. No matter how many blankets were heaped on me, I couldn't get warm enough. I quaked with bitterness while rats and snakes in the walls scratched and clawed away. It sounded like they were marching inside the walls while getting ready to fight each other to the death. This went on every night and it was clear to me Grandma and Grandpa were accustomed to the racket. I'd look over at them sleeping like nobody's business, oblivious to the sounds that made me crawl beneath the covers and not want to come out. Grandma told me those scurrying little creatures had been living in the walls since she and Grandpa moved into this old place. She said, "If you don' mess with them, they wont mess with you 'cause they live here too."

My feelings of abandonment and loss unleashed a waterfall of tears. From out of nowhere, an angry storm blew in, mirroring what I was feeling inside myself.

Wind battered the house and lashes of rain whipped across the roof. A deep, groaning sound rose and fell. The rain pounded on the metal roof like it was punching tiny holes through the tin. I wanted to crawl under the bed, but I was afraid of what might be under there. That was the worst night of my life. When I woke the next morning, I rushed outside to see the damage from the storm. I was amazed that everything was still intact – even the chickens were still milling around the yard doing their thing. I was hoping that one of those bouts of wind would have swept their little butts right off the face of the earth.

Those first few nights I cried myself to sleep. The cold was unbearable. My body convulsed like I was having a seizure. I tried to remember Detroit and the family I was stripped away from. I couldn't conjure any faces- only silhouettes all in shadowy shades of gray. I had no recollection of my mother. Each day that had gone by since I left, what little I did remember about my mother's voice and face was slowly but surely slipping away. I had no way to articulate how deeply this scared me.

I continued to wrestle with the cold until Grandma got up in the middle of the night and placed a quilt on top of the other quilts already covering me. I couldn't move. I felt a sense of unimaginable comfort. For the first time in days, I relaxed. Swaddled like an infant in a receiving blanket. It didn't make sense, but that quilt engulfed me in a feeling of bliss- the smell and all its colors- reds and blues reflecting in the firelight. I didn't notice the quilt had missing pieces, barely hanging on its backing. To me, it was dazzling with cloths of soft prints, gaudy corduroys, stripes and plaids, and every other pattern you could imagine. That old quilt had personality and from the moment Grandma laid it on my bed, I claimed it as my own.

CHAPTER 2
GHOSTS AND HAINTS

I stood in the front yard inside a palpable silence. Everything was woods, woods and more woods. The pine and sycamore trees were as tall as the sky. My grandparents' front yard was huge, with flowering plants abounding– honeysuckle, black-eyed Susans, beds of yellow, pink, red and white roses, and the ones that were my favorite: the four o'clock flowers- magnificent crimson blooms that only opened their buds at four in the afternoon. I'd sit and watch as they erupted into a panacea of blossoms. The grandeur of Grandma's flower garden suppressed some of my sadness.

As I sat on the concrete stoop taking it all in, Grandpa's voice rang in my ear. "Whatcha doin' ov'r thar gal?" There he was, sitting in his rocker under the old oak tree chewing on a twig. "You hongry'? Lula gone fix somethin' teat' direc'ly." Out of the corner of my eye, I saw Grandma making her way down the dogtrot – a long open hallway down the middle of the house that separated our bedroom from the front room. She was belting out one of her old Negro spirituals that sent shivers right through my spine.

After a breakfast of oversized homemade biscuits, apple preserves and grits, Grandma proclaimed that she thought I had a tapeworm. "You ain't knee high to a duck's behind, jus' don' know where you puttin' all that food. Grandma think you got a tapeworm or somethin'."

Grandpa howled with laughter. Watching him laugh with a mouthful of biscuits and grits spraying clear across the table was amusing. It sent me into an endless giggling fit.

My grandparents' house was casting a spell on me. Even though there was a lot I couldn't get used to, there was a mystique to that old place. Above the fireplace in the bedroom was Grandma's photograph collection neatly displayed on the mantelpiece. It was a private world of untold stories.

There were ones of families who looked like they came from long ago, dressed funny and stiffly posed. There were children with dirty faces and scuffed-up clothes. Then there was one I particularly loved: a striking black woman named Leontyne Price, an opera singer whose mother sang in the church choir with Grandma back in Laurel, Mississippi. Grandma proudly lifted up a photo of a wealthy looking White family with a robust man and a fiery red-haired lady. Two little girls kneeled on the floor beside them. She read aloud the inscription on the bottom: "We will always love you, Miss Lula." "I prac'ly raise these chil'ren," Grandma said.

The dogtrot was set up as a living room area. There was a picture hanging from its papered walls that commanded the whole space. It was of a tall, remarkable woman in a long white dress and matching hat. She was larger than life itself. Of all the photographs, that one intrigued me the most. Grandma said it was her sister, Ella. Her eyes were captivating and had a piercing stare. I wanted to know more about her.

The most magical room of all was Grandma's front room, which was off limits to me. I was strictly forbidden to go in unless I was with my grandparents. There was a sofa and an antique chifferobe that was kept locked with a long metal key that Grandma had in her apron pocket. My eyes got wide as saucers as she unlocked the cabinet and pulled out a glass plate filled with homemade teacakes. Grandma shook her head as she watched me devour two cookies at record speed. I tried to peek in to see what other delights she had stored in there, but she put the key back in the lock and shut the door.

What other treasures lay behind those doors? Just like the bedroom, the front room had a fireplace and a mantle adorned with pictures in rustic frames. I was struck by one of an older couple. The woman looked just like Grandpa with her high cheekbones, fair skin and sharp nose. The man standing behind her was a distinguished looking gentleman with dark silky skin. He wore a starched collared shirt under a gray suit. "That be your granddaddy Edgar's mama Alice and papa Josh. They with the Lord now."

My curiosity got the better of me and I decided when Grandma retreated to the kitchen to start supper, I was going to sneak into the front room. Something that was forbidden only piqued my interest more. I was on a mission to discover the secrets locked behind those cabinet doors. I swear I heard that room personally invite me in to explore its unknown.

As Grandma made her way to where the kitchen sat way in the back of the house, down the long dogtrot, out of view, I was off on my adventure. I stood there soaking up the thrill of being in a forbidden paradise. I looked over at the sofa and it beckoned me to sit on it. It was covered in hard plastic so when I lifted one of my bare legs, it stuck to it, making a crackling sound as it released me from its grip. I giggled and relished in a few minutes of lifting my legs up and down just to hear that crackle.

I got up and went over to the chifferobe. I poked a stick into the keyhole. To my surprise, the door swung wide open on its own. It was unlocked! What a stroke of luck! I climbed up so I could scan the contents of this massive wooden albatross. My eyes were heat-seeking missiles as I honed in on two round red and green metal tins inside. I pulled them down from the shelf. Inside the green one were pressed flowered handkerchiefs and a handful of silver and gold coins. As I struggled to remove the lid from the red one, it popped open and all its contents came flying out. Black and white photographs tumbled all over the floor. I saw a picture of Grandma smiling and holding hands with someone. I was just about to start picking them up when Grandma walked into the room. There I stood with an open tin in my hot little hands and photographs scattered all around. She looked as shocked to see me, as I was to see her. I regretted not scoring another of those teacakes before I was caught.

Grandma didn't scold me, but pointed to my great grandparents' Alice and Josh's picture on the mantle and said, "Papa Josh and Mama Alice's spirit live in this here room. You can mess 'roun in here and break somethin' if you want. They are haints in here and them spirits'll chase you outta here. Now gone. I'll clean up this here mess you done made, Lord Jesus."

I discovered that ghost stories abound down in the country. Most of the old folks believed in spirits. Getting busted cold by Grandma, I probably looked more like a ghost than Papa Josh and Mama Alice ever could. Having my great-grandparents' spirits chasing after me made me shake in my shoes. Grandma being disappointed in my behavior was vexing to my spirit. I didn't want to be sent away again.

I retreated to the screened-in front porch that overlooked the front yard. It was my favorite part of the house. The long wooden swing was my perch. I stretched out with my legs cocked up over the back for hours, fantasizing about Detroit and at what point those 'haints' were going to attack my little behind. The swing hung from two half-rusted chains that clanked and clattered as it swayed back and forth.

As I lay on my "pity pot," Grandpa slowly made his way over from the front yard. He took a seat in one of the rocking chairs. "I jus' come to see whut all dat co'motion 'bout. You cryin' agin? Come ov'r heah li'l Black gal." I was too young to question what grownups said or what words they used. All I heard was the tenderness of his tone. I sat on his knee as he rocked me in the chair. "Nigh, you know whut, li'l gal, I be headin' to town tomorry. I'll see whether Lula let ya go wit me. Nigh draw up dem tears, trouble don' las' always."

Grandpa was a quiet man, but he laughed and smiled a lot. He hadn't talked much since I arrived, but when he did, it was in a low whisper. He had what Grandma called an awful case of 'Uncle Arthur,' which I learned was arthritis. No wonder Grandpa shuffled along at a crawl. Grandma hounded him for being "as slow as molasses." I swear it took him an hour to get from the front yard to the front porch. Grandpa had many other ailments including difficulty hearing. He seemed to get a kick out of Grandma's little one and two liners. He'd shake his head, laugh and come back with, "I'm a comin' Miss Lula." Even though he didn't talk much, he made it up with laughter; I found it hilarious that he'd laugh at things that weren't funny. I'd make funny faces just to see if he'd laugh at my stupidity, and sure enough, he always did. We spent hours whooping and hollering over nothing.

The sun began to set as Grandma made her way to the front porch. She had finished making Sunday dinner, even though it was Saturday evening. Because Grandma didn't believe in doing any cleaning, cooking, farming or anything else on Sunday, she made Sunday's meal the night before. It was enough food to feed an army. As she plopped down in the rocking chair, she looked worn out. Her apron was filled with residue from the meal she just prepared and her socks had fallen down around her ankles. She used the bottom of her apron to wipe the sweat of the Alabama heat from her face. I guess either Grandma had forgiven me for trespassing in the forbidden front room or she felt I'd learned my lesson. She never mentioned it again.

"Come here gal, Grandma gone teach you how to lif' dandruff." She reached in her apron pocket and pulled out an old black comb that was missing half its teeth. I sat and watched as she parted her hair until her scalp was showing. She started digging into it with the part of the comb that still had teeth. "You see jus' part and scratch, part and scratch. Now you do it. You ain't gone hurt Grandma, chile." As she leaned her head back, I began doing what she told me. Before long, her hair was raining snow at the roots, white flakes cascading down to the ground. As I stood there lifting Grandma's dandruff, she hummed the most angelic melody I'd ever heard. I could have fallen asleep standing right there on the front porch scratching Grandma's hair, but I got distracted by the cola Grandpa brought back from his last trip to town.

Cola was one of the only things we didn't grow. Sipping on it was a treat, but Grandma never allowed me to drink it from the bottle; she'd make a big pitcher of ice tea and pour in a couple of bottles of cola to enhance the flavor. I hated when she did this and I hated ice tea. All I kept thinking was: what a waste of a good bottle of cola.

Whenever I'd get too full of myself and complain about not having treats and luxuries that other kids back in Detroit had, Grandma would nip it right in the bud. Nothing was ever a simple yes or no answer. She had a story for everything. She'd launch into long detailed diatribes about people's lives from long ago. She'd relate these stories to whatever was going on with me at the time. Sometimes I wanted to kick myself for asking a question or making a comment because her stories went on forever. I'd listen to her talk about people being worse off than us- folks starving, slavery days, and her parents, who didn't have a pot to piss in, or a window to throw it out of. "That's why you don' nev'r get so high on your horse, 'cause it's a mighty long way from the saddle to the ground."

CHAPTER 3

TOWN OF LIVINGSTON

There was a spring that ran about seven hundred feet from my grandparents' front yard. We used the water for bathing during the summer months when we didn't get rain. Occasionally, Grandma told me to go fetch her and Grandpa a cold drink from that spring during those hot days sitting around in the front yard.

The dead of summer had arrived. It seemed a hundred years since I was dropped at my grandparents' doorstep. I was living up to my country girl status, as Grandma put it months ago. I loved drawing small buckets of water from the creek because it was so blue; the sound it made as it travelled over the rocks was music to my ears. I'd sit for hours listening. That was my time not to have a care in the world until I'd hear Grandma calling out for me to come home. She yelled so loud you could hear the echo of my name bouncing off the sycamore trees.

In my rush to get back up the hill to the house, half of the water spilled from my pail. Grandma would chuckle and say, "Gal, you ain't got 'nough water here to feed chickens lest long to fill me and your grandpa's glasses. Now you jus' gone have to go on back down to that creek and lick the calf ov'r." I'd think about all the sayings that Grandma threw out at me. Most didn't make any sense at all. They were probably truisms passed down from her parents, developed during slavery and derived from trying to grasp an unknown language.

Our house was so far out in the country that you could hear a car coming from miles away. At night, you could see the headlights before hearing the engine. Since it was wooded, with no streetlights – the nearest neighbors were relatives, living about two miles away- everything was pitch black; the lights from the car would gradually illuminate the darkness until they disappeared.

I didn't see an automobile more than about once a month. Riding in one was another thing – that was a real treat because it was far and few in between. My cousin Jeff, Miss Sugar and Aunt Honey Bee were the only people in the country I knew that owned one. Jeff had an old, beat up blue truck that ran smooth. He'd pick up Grandpa and take him to downtown Livingston about once a month. Usually Grandma wouldn't let me go because I had chores, and she had quilts to complete. She made so many quilts in her lifetime, her long, thin fingers were riffed with callouses. She continued to accept orders from well-to-do Livingston families, and for family and friends. I loved working on the quilts with her. It seemed like I just held and fetched, but Grandma acted like she couldn't have done it without my help. It was a salve for my aching heart.

One of my jobs was to gather wood chips for the fire. Grandma boiled water outside in a cast iron pot on a roaring fire. Once the water boiled, she and Grandpa slowly dipped the quilt into scalding water. I was too little to help around the open flame so I'd watch as they dipped the quilt in quickly, pull it out with walking sticks and heave them onto the line. Grandma said the boiling water helped seal the stitches into the fabric. Sometimes folks would pick up their quilts, and other times, Grandpa would take them to town when he went on his monthly visit to Millen's store. These times were mainly used for Grandpa to 'shoot the bobo' with those old White men who sat around Millen's.

Grandma could make quilts from any kind of cloth given to her. Folks would bring new cloth on large spools made of various textures, but that wasn't her preference. If the person brought cloth from old, used clothes, Grandma wanted to know whether or not the person who owned them had passed on. Most knew of her superstitions about the cloth. I couldn't understand Grandma's reason for not using the clothes of living people. Whenever I asked, she'd say, "b'cause it ain't a death cloth, chile." According to her, the cloth of the dead made the quilt come alive for the person who owned it. If folks wrapped themselves in the quilt, the spirit of all those souls would come alive and watch over them.

One day Grandma announced I was going to town with Grandpa. I was so elated I could barely sleep the night before. It didn't take much to get me excited. I acted like this would be the last ride of my life. I could've been making a trip straight to hell, but I didn't care as long as I got to ride out of those woods and see other parts of the world. The caveat: I wouldn't be getting anywhere near Cousin Jeff's truck until all my chores were spic and span.

Most of the kids in Detroit would probably consider the things I had to do as repulsive. Many of them would probably run away from home and never look back if they had to take out the slop jar. I never got used to doing this. The best way to describe the slop jar is one simple phrase: shoveling shit. It was a large white metal container with a lid on it that sat on the floor next to the bed.

Slop jars were only supposed to be used for "number ones"- in other words, peeing. If you wanted to poo, you were supposed to take yourself to the outhouse, in the middle of the cotton field. The rule was different for Grandpa Edgar. Since he had the piles, he did his business in the slop jar because Grandma said, "When you gotta go, you gotta go."

Grandpa went often and usually at night. That was nasty for me the next morning. Between the vile stench of Grandpa's poop and urine, I was double-whammed.

One day, I decided that if Grandpa did his business at night, I'd do the same. I hated going to the outhouse in the dark. It was scary. Well, Grandma wasn't having any of that! She didn't have to pull the switch on me very often; one of her infamous looks and not a word needed to be spoken. I got the "you ain't grown folk" lecture. Needless to say, I never made that mistake again, but whenever I could, I'd sneak out and do my business in the cotton fields. I'd take that soft cotton over that hard ass newspaper any old day.

Once I finished that vile chore, I had to complete my other chore, which was just as bad. I had to make the daily trek under the house to look for eggs. My grandparents' house was no different from the neighbors' houses. They all sat on cinder blocks far enough off the ground for a normal sized person to crawl under on their knees. Since I was small, I had a lot of space. Grandma had a lot of chickens. She made it clear as day that if I didn't crawl under that house and get those eggs, I wouldn't be going to town. To me, chickens were the most evasive little creatures on the face of the earth and Grandma knew I detested them. I was convinced they felt the same about me, but I was bigger than them and determined to get their eggs one way or the other. Those little varmints were the enemy and the only thing standing between me and going to downtown Livingston.

It was something about that mother hen! She ignored me and refused to come off that nest. It was black as coal under that house and I was covered in bird shit from head to toe. Mother hen didn't care about that. She just looked at me cocking her head to the side. Through the darkness, all I could see was her beady eyes. If chickens could talk, she would've been laughing at me. She wasn't going to budge. She spread her wings wider, puffing out her chest to protect her eggs at all costs.

I was determined to get my hot little hands on them. We fought. She won.

I ran to Grandma screaming and crying at the top of my lungs. I didn't know whether I was angry at the chicken or upset with myself for screwing around with the beast that threatened my ride into town. Letting that mama hen get the best of me was probably one of the lowest points of my life thus far. Grandma consoled me and told me it was all right. I thought she might give me a reprieve for the day, but that wasn't Grandma's way.

She went to the back porch, got a dry ear of corn, and kneaded off a handful of kernels. She put them in my tiny hand and closed my fingers around them so they wouldn't drop. She told me to take that corn and use it to tempt the hen off her nest. I hesitated going back under the house, but Grandma kept repeating in that old country drawl, "Gone now, gone girl." Having no choice in the matter, I went back under the house with the corn and sure enough, that old hen went after it. In turn, I went after the eggs. The chicken and I both ended up happy.

I learned a valuable lesson that day about perseverance and never giving up. I bathed the chicken crap off me in the large silver tub in the backyard. The water was cold, but I was so glad to be going into town, I barely noticed. Even Grandma's homemade lye soap didn't burn my eyes as much. I wore my little plaid dress and Grandma braided my hair into one that sat on the top of my head and two smaller ones on either side. If being beaten by a chicken was a low point of my young life, then riding in the back of Cousin Jeff's truck was one of the highlights.

With the wind blowing up my nose and down my throat, I felt free as a bird. I stood up like I was an airplane ready to take off and soar through the air. My mind was somewhere far away until Grandpa beat on the back window for me to sit down. I loved bouncing around in the truck because my little body wasn't heavy enough to stay balanced. Every dip in the road sent me flying into fits of laughter. As the truck weaved its way up and down hills and valleys, I felt like I was on a roller coaster. My stomach did summersaults. I didn't care if we went to town or not. I just wanted more of that belly-bouncing laughter.

Along the way, we stopped by to see Mrs. Mary, a well-off White woman who lived on the outskirts of Livingston. Grandpa wanted to drop off the quilt that Grandma had made for her and finished the day before. The quilt was alit with beautiful bright colors. It had a blue and white border and the inside alternated between red and green, with a sunburst of yellow radiating out from its middle. It looked like the sun dropped right out of the sky and landed on it. I loved watching Grandma put the finishing touches on it; all those colors coexisting together without clashing one bit. Grandma had a way of turning old, worn out clothes into a work of art that people would travel miles just to marvel at.

Mrs. Mary looked like the female version of the Pillsbury doughboy. She was as white as a sheep with a big squishy stomach. I had to restrain myself from poking my finger in her belly to see if she'd make that silly giggle like on the commercial. She unfolded the quilt and stretched it out along the length of her sofa. Her pasty face turned blood red as she began to sob uncontrollably. I stood there "like a knot on a log," as Grandma would say. She went on and on about how Grandma had brought to life the parents she tragically lost long ago, when she was a child. Her deceased parent's clothes were transformed into sunshine. As we drove away, Mrs. Mary stood in the doorway of her white frame house, clutching her quilt like her parents had come back to life and were standing right there with her.

When we arrived in town, the first thing I saw was a giant brick courthouse. It sat on the square, swallowing up the other buildings with its hugeness. Succulent flowers of every color surrounded it in a fence of blossoms. Two water fountains sat right below the steps with 'Colored' and 'White' signs hanging from wrought iron hooks. When we got out of the truck, Grandpa gave me a stern lecture. "Don' let me catcha nowheres 'round that cotehouse, ya heah me gal? If you wants water, you drank 'til you bust from dis jar right heah." Grandpa brought a big mason jar filled to the brim with water and ice. I didn't understand why something so beautiful caused so much ire from Grandpa.

I found out later about the atrocities that Blacks suffered in and around that courthouse. Many cases were overturned after a lynching and the guilty parties, who were White, were set free. Some of the victims were people my grandparents knew. That courthouse represented hatred and reminded Grandpa of the racism and bigotry that existed in Livingston.

Millen's General Store was *the* store in town: a large one-story frame building with a big porch. There were rocking chairs where old men "liked to sit 'round and tell lies," according to Grandma. Inside, in the middle of the racks of merchandise, was an old black stove where folks sat in the wintertime. Cousin Jeff left us there to go off on his own errands.

When Grandpa walked up, they welcomed him like he was an old hand and moved over so he could sit in *his* chair. They asked him if he'd brought any of Grandma's delicious teacakes with him. "Naw, not dis time." Several of the men were White, but no one seemed to care. They talked about hunting and fishing, and Josh Horn, Grandpa's daddy, a local legend who taught these old men how to hunt and tell ghost stories. They told blood-curdling tales that Great Grandpa Josh told them on their hunting expeditions. Grandpa liked hearing stories about his papa. The stories were about ghost riders and headless dogs. They spooked me silly. Spirits were everywhere in the country.

I was feeling uneasy when I heard a walking stick strike the floor. I turned to see an old White woman with curly gray hair in a spastic frizz on her head. She wore a faded print dress and shoes with heels like giant black bricks. I hurried out of the way so she wouldn't step on me with those clunky shoes. She loudly pronounced, "GOOD AFTERNOON," then told the young man sitting next to Grandpa, "Clint, move your ass out the way." She sat down and with a wide grin, turned to Grandpa and said, "Hey there, Edgar." Grandpa smiled and said, "Evening, Miss Ruby." It was Ruby Tartt.

Grandpa told her I was his granddaughter. She said, "Somebody get that little gal a cola, what's wrong with you all?" I sat there grinning like a fool. Miss Ruby took over the conversation, becoming louder and more animated. She knew all of Great Grandpa Josh's stories, not just the ghost stories. She liked to tell the ones about his life with his wife, Alice, which I loved. When she told a story it was as if I was right there living it. I devoured every word that came out of her mouth.

Watching Miss Ruby was fascinating. Everyone dipped snuff, but she had her own unique way. Her right arm was barely mobile, planted next to her body. She took a long pause to gather her thoughts, pulling her bottom lip away from her teeth with two fingers of her bad hand. She held the jar of snuff with her good hand so a portion could drop right into the open space behind her lip. You could see a lump in her chin where the snuff was. She wiped the juices that dripped off her chin with the back of her hand, and picked up the story where she left off.

When she finished, everyone burst into lively conversation. Grandpa was more wound up than I'd ever seen him. Snuff drizzled down the front of *his* chin as he spoke. All the folks sitting there had a little knot protruding from their chins. There was a rusty can beside each rocking chair for spitting snuff. It was as nasty as that old slop jar. I placed my tongue under my bottom lip wanting to know what it felt like to have a snuff knot. Grandpa pointed at me, laughed, and told the others I was "tryin' to act grown." They all thought that was funny. I ducked my head in embarrassment. I didn't want Miss Ruby to think I was childish.

Grandpa and Ruby Tartt got up and walked around the store. When Miss Ruby came back, she handed me a brown paper bag. I opened it excitedly and discovered an entire rainbow of ribbons. I thought I'd throw up right in that bag. I hoped Miss Ruby didn't see the disgust on my face, but I think she did. She said she hoped I'd grow up to be smart like my great-grandpa Josh. I was taught that when you addressed an adult, it was always "Yes, ma'am," or "No, ma'am," or "sir," and you thanked the person. "Yes, ma'am," I said, and thanked her. She nodded and left.

Grandpa had an account at that store because the Millen's, who were part of the local White gentry, and the Horns, Grandpa's family, were related in a particular way. Grandpa was part of what was called the "hushed bloodline," meaning Old Man Millen, a White man, and my grandfather were related. Grandpa came down from the bloodline of White Millen's a ways back. No one ever mentioned it, but everybody knew.

That White blood was passed down through his mama Alice's lineage. The Tartt's and Millen's were mixed up in Alice's bloodline. No one knew exactly who Alice's father was. All anyone knew was that Alice came into the world as a result of "ol' masta creepin'." Her mother was said to have been either Native American or Spanish, but no one knew for sure.

Grandpa Edgar and his fifteen brothers and sisters were light-skinned or, as his sister, Aunt Bessie would say, "Light, bright and damn near white." Anybody with eyes could see from the picture in the front room that Great Grandpa Josh was a dark skinned man. This didn't stop him from objecting when Grandpa Edgar wanted to marry Grandma Lula, who was also dark skinned. Grandpa paid him no mind and married Grandma anyway. He was in love.

On the way home from town, we stopped on the outskirts of Livingston at an old farmhouse. It resembled my grandparents' house, except it had a room that sat above the front porch, with a window facing the front yard. What was strange about this house was there was a mattress hanging out the window, slung over the window-sill. Sheets and quilts draped over the fence that stretched around the house. Colorful quilts looked eerily familiar to Grandma Lula's. I couldn't figure out why all their bedding was hanging around outside, including that mattress in the window.

As I hopped down from Cousin Jeff's truck bed, Grandpa motioned for me to stay out in the front yard with the other two children, who looked about my age. They were sitting in the yard dressed up in their Sunday-looking clothes. The boy sat in one of the chairs with his feet barely touching the ground. He kicked sand and pebbles in the air with his Sunday church-shoes. The girl laughed every time the dirt and rocks flew up in the air. I joined in on the laughter not because it was funny, but because I wanted to be part of the hoopla.

With one eye on these bad-ass children and one eye trying to find out what Grandpa was doing in the house, I decided I needed to sneak away. I peered through the front door down the long dogtrot so I could investigate what was going on inside. I'd spent so much time around grown folks that these childish games did nothing for me. There were bigger fish to fry inside.

As I darted out of the front yard, I heard the boy yell, "I'm gonna tell," but I ignored him. I was tempted to crawl under the house to see if I could get a better view of the backyard, but unlike my grandparents' place, I wasn't familiar with the underbelly or what might've been lurking in the dark crevices. I walked down the long hallway to find Grandpa. I'd deal with the consequences later.

As I stepped into the hall, I came face to face with a man lying on a long board. He was wearing a white shirt and a black bow tie. I wondered why he was sleeping. I hoped he wasn't mad at me for coming in his house without knocking. Like Grandma's hallway, there were a vast array of pictures that graced the walls; flowers and plants strategically placed on shelves. I felt like I was in a flower garden. Just as I was ready to go back and get more face time with the sleeping man, Grandpa and an older lady appeared from one of the rooms. That was the loudest I had ever heard Grandpa raise his voice.

"Get ov'r heah gal!" I ran over to where he stood. He took his hand and slapped me on my backside. I ran away crying like nobody's business and jumped on the back of Cousin Jeff's truck. He was sitting in the driver's seat and must've seen me crying my eyes out. I told him about getting 'whupped' because I went into the house where that man was sleeping. Cousin Jeff, who appeared aloof most of the time, busted out laughing like I was the biggest fool in the world. He said, "Chile, t'waint no man sleepin' in nair. Dat was a dead man on de coolin' board waitin' fo' de sun to go down so his spirit be carried away. Lord Chile, you a mess." He bellowed out another round of laughter. This was my first encounter with a dead person.

I hurled myself into the truck and balled up into a fetus, my little ass shaking like I'd been dropped in an ice bucket. I must've dozed off because when I woke up, Grandpa was standing at the back of the truck calling out for me. "Hey gal, get on down heah chile and get dis ice cream." Grandpa was all smiles, so he must've forgotten about what happened. We sat around in the front yard- me, Grandpa, the folks in that house, and the kids dressed in Sunday clothes. We ate homemade vanilla ice cream until dusk.

I couldn't wait to jump in the back of the truck and begin the journey home. It started to rain a light drizzle and I was content listening to the katydids and crickets as we drove along the dirt road past the cotton and cornfields.

Grandma was standing at the front gate with her big apron and arms wide open, ready to hear about my day. Even though it'd only been a few hours, I felt like I hadn't seen Grandma in weeks. Grandpa told her about my run-in with the corpse. Grandma explained how that man had been laid out on the "cooling board" because he died the day before. She said when a person died inside of a house you have to hang the mattress, sheets, and quilts that were on the bed, outside until the sun went down. This allowed the sun's shadow to pass over the dead person. If not, his spirit would forever roam, unable to rest in peace. My young mind couldn't grasp the concept of death. All I knew was if Grandma said it, it must be real.

CHAPTER 4
COURAGEOUS ELLA

G randma sat down behind me on the concrete stoop. She reached into her apron pocket and pulled out the same half toothless comb that I used to lift her dandruff. This comb had a lot of mileage on it. She scraped my hair while singing:

> *"This little light of mine*
> *I'm gonna let it shine*
> *Let it shine, let it shine, let it shine."*

Each time the comb stroked my scalp all the worries of my little world were raked away. Tears fell from my eyes, not from pain or loneliness, but from the melodious notes that floated off Grandma's lips. I could've sat there forever.

We began a regular pattern of spending long country days sewing quilts while Grandma told stories that were as soothing to me as her singing. We usually worked on quilts under the oak tree in the front. One afternoon, Grandma decided it was time to repair my quilt. It still had missing pieces and some of the cloth was dangling by threads. I was going to have to give up my quilt, my beloved quilt, while it was being fixed. I hadn't been without it since the moment I claimed it as mine. Grandma said, "It's high time we finish it. Been long 'nough."

I closed my eyes and imaged what it would look like once Grandma worked her magic on it. Now that I was the focus of her attention, I started feeling special. I'd never felt special in all my life. Grandma dug around in her bag of rags and pulled out a piece of faded off-white cloth, smiling like she'd found a long-lost treasure. She started humming one of her sweet tunes. She held up the faded white cloth and told me it was from Ella's wedding dress. Ella was the woman whose portrait graced the hallway and whom I longed to know more about. I'd finally be learning about her that day. "This here the firs' cloth we puttin' in your quilt," Grandma said.

That was the beginning of a history lesson that would stick with me for the rest of my life. The folktales of my ancestors and Grandma's friends who were born in the late 1800's would be the layers of used clothes that laid the foundation for my quilt. Each piece portrayed the story of that person's life and death. It wasn't only their garment that would embed into my quilt, it was their stories and what they were able to achieve regardless of the insurmountable obstacles they faced. Grandma had many memories of times past. She'd refer to those days as "after slavery times," or "during slavery times." It became her way of measuring the span of her lifetime.

Ella's story was an interlude to the tales spun about the quilt. Grandma would stop intermittently to bark out, "You payin' 'tention chile?" This was her way of letting me know how important these stories were and how they were intimately attached to her past. I felt honored she was passing them down to me. She told me how each piece of cloth was married to the misery and pain of those whose lives had come to a sudden tragic end many years ago. While other children learned and memorized the fictitious stories of "The Three Little Pigs", and "Little Red Riding Hood," I was being taught real-life stories; ones of hardship, loss, love, courage, and strength. Stories about how the making of a quilt had impact. You could stitch broken pieces of the heart back together and mend it somehow.

I'd gasp when I picked up material that still showed signs of being soiled, some with human blood. The stains were so set in that even soap and water couldn't remove them. They were forever embedded into the fibers of the fabric. I was sure some were stained with sweat from pushing the plow and working the fields from sunup to sundown. Some cloths bore the tears of heartache from loss and abandonment, emotions I understood.

Those were the cloths that were used to mend and finish my quilt. Grandma was meticulous as she stitched each individual piece together. Like finding the exact piece to a puzzle. She'd measure each one with the length of her hand to ensure a perfect fit.

It was with those cloths that Grandma built a colorful masterpiece. Something so tattered turned whole again, into a cherished possession people could wrap themselves up in.

When Grandma stitched, she went into a kind of a trance. It's what folks down South called a 'stitchin' rhythm.' As she began her story, she spoke with deep conviction. It commanded my full attention, and my full attention is what I gave.

"I'm gonna tell you the story of my sistah Ella," she said. "'Tis a well-known fac' that even though the north won the war, they sure didn' let on 'bout it down here in the south too much. Now, there was a man name ol' Masta Young who live in those days down in Laurel, Miss'sippi. He have a big plantation with a lot of slaves. He was the meanes' slave owner in the state of Miss'sippi, jus' plain ol' hateful. Mama say he beat his slaves comin' and goin'. Not a day go by he come out that big ol' house that sit square dead on top of Dev'ls Hill. You can hear him b'fore you see him comin' 'cause he breathin' like he done plow forty acres and truth be told, he couldn' hit a lick at a snake. But he sure know how to make Mama and Papa's life not worth livin' mornin' 'til night. My folks, Joe and Emma Young, they was own by that sorry dev'l."

"B'fore the war was ov'r, while the slaves was still slaves, Mama had four chil'ren. That ev'l Masta Young take those chil'ren and sell them 'way; sell ev'ry last one of them, some of them still nursin'. I know it like to kill Mama." Grandma shook her head in disgust. I felt her pain. She wasn't born yet at the time of the story, but said Emma passed it on to her when she was younger than I was. Her voice trailed off as she talked and stitched in perfect rhythm. I watched as the white thread moved in and out of the fabric without missing a beat.

Grandma would repeat the same stories over and over again. Nothing ever changed; the names, the people, the environment. It was like learning my mathematics table and the alphabet, repetitively until it became rote. I was sure that was why the tales of the quilt ingrained deep into my consciousness and never left. I thought Grandma was doing that on purpose. Oral histories and the passing down of ancestral stories were a crucial and fundamental piece that existed in the Black culture. At some point, the importance of cultural storytelling disappeared, no longer considered to be of any value. Grandma was passing those stories down to me so that her history wouldn't be lost.

"Ol' Masta Young die, praise the Lord. 'Twas right after the Surrender. Then commence to pass down to his son, the young Mr. Young. He the spittin' image of his papa, potbelly and all, but his mean streak was a li'l smaller. Lots of the ex-slaves stay on, I reckon since the ol' man was gone. Our mama and papa, Joe and Emma, stay on, too. Then there a gift from God: Ella was born to Emma and Joe, 'round 'bout 1868 or '69. They mighty happy 'bout that. There was somethin' special 'bout Ella. She born with a veil ov'r her face."

The veil was a sack that coated the baby's face. Grandma said it was believed to be an omen and happened only rarely. It was said to indicate mysterious powers and great fortune to all. "B'fore we cleant her off, Joe take that veil and lay it out to dry. When it commence to dryin', Mama and Papa make sure the sun don' go down on it. Mama say that take 'way Ella's gift if night fall on it. When it dry all out, Papa Joe make it so Ella can wear it 'round her neck fo' good luck. 'Til today, we still don' know what came of Ella's good luck piece." She said Ella was gifted, but wasn't sure if the veil was a blessing or a curse.

"That fac' spread like wildfire, and soon ev'rybody from fifty miles 'round know 'bout it. Young Mr. Young in the big house sure 'nough heard 'bout it. He had the consumption, just like Edgar, only his real bad and he hardly breathe at all. Fac', he come close to death many a time so he thought he better make right sure that baby stay near to hand."

"He call Papa Joe up to the big house and of'ered him some land where he can farm and live in the li'l house that used to be the ol' slave quarters. Papa Joe have to pay for the land after each crop, in 'stallments. He so glad to get his own land he 'greed to it right then and there. It come to be that Ella grow up workin' in the Young's house like no Colored girl ev'r did b'fore. Li'l did Papa Joe know that ev'l plan young Mr. Young cook up would tear my fam'ly ev'ry which a way."

Grandma described what it was like in Mississippi back then. "Some White folk wont let slav'ry die. You seen it ev'rywheres; the beatin's, the raids by the Ku Kluxers, and them lynchin's. So many Coloreds kil't at Black Bottom Creek, the name of that place was changed to cov'r the shame." Grandma recounted how some Black families were shielded from persecution because they were secretly related to prominent White families due to 'ol' masta creepin'.' There was only so much protection that could be had in those days.

"The young Mr. Young was blood relation to Sheriff Renfro, who come down to visit the Young's. Jus' to think, he come all the way ov'r from Alabama where he live jus' so he can sit on the front porch and mess with the Colored help that live and work on the plantation. The Sheriff all the time givin' the young Mr. Young an earful on how to treat his Coloreds. He 'specially had a lot to say 'bout Ella. Ella wont keep her head down and she wont gone act humble neither. She had that Sheriff all riled up, he didn' know whether he was comin' or goin'. She go into that big house when she want, sailin' right through that front door, fine as you please, thank you, ma'am, jus' like White folk. She walk in and all the Colored help lif' they heads and take notice."

"They be a bustle all through the house. Missus Young kinda set her up ov'r them. Sheriff Renfro filled young Mr. Young head with all kinda hateful talk 'bout Ella. But the young Mr. Young, he needed Ella, and he jus' let it all roll off his back. He need Ella 'cause our mama, Emma, teach Ella all 'bout herbs and healin' plants. Emma learnt it from her mama. Emma and Ella got plants from out the woods and brew up a special concoction fo' the young Mr. Young, and fix up a plaster fo' him. Ella come in ev'ry mornin' to his study and make him sit still there in his chair while she put the plaster on his chest and make him drink the herbal concoction. His breathin' clear up like no man's bizness. He breathin' jus' as free and clear as I sittin' here tellin' you 'bout it. As time roll 'round pract'ly no spell at all."

Grandma said that at the same time, his business was booming. He became one of the largest producers of cotton and timber in Laurel. He couldn't believe his good fortune. Having Ella on the plantation was the best thing that had ever happened to him. Things were going along just fine.

At that moment, Grandpa poked his head out the front door and spoke in that voice just above a whisper, "Miss Lula, I need some of dat lini'ment and sulfur." Grandma put down her sewing and rushed into the house. I knew this meant that Grandpa was having one of his spells, just like the young Mr. Young. Grandma went in to make him a plaster concoction to ease *his* breathing. This also meant that the rest of the story of Ella was going to have to wait.

CHAPTER 5

BETHEL HILL

Just as I was getting adjusted to life in the country, I found out I'd be starting school. Summer was almost over. In those days, there was no kindergarten. You went right into the first grade. I didn't think too much about it since the end of the summer was still a few weeks away. There was nothing to me that indicated school was right around the corner. Even though the memory of when I climbed into the back seat of that old black car was long since fading, I still recalled times spent with my family, especially with my sisters. After all, the three of us had slept together in the same bed. You can't get much closer than that.

Back in Detroit, my sisters would come home with bags of clothes from the local Goodwill Store. I'd watch as they tried on every garment, spinning around in the mirror admiring themselves in their new used duds. I hated when my sisters went off to school. I felt abandoned. I struggled to remember what transpired on the days my sisters left me. The only memory I had was of them running out the front door and the screen slamming behind them. I couldn't recall anything from the time they left for school until the time they returned. It was all a blur.

I imagined me and my brothers were left with my mother, who was probably tired from the long hours of working nights, especially after having eight children; four of them "stair-step" and a set of twins. It must've been tiring for my mother, barely thirty with a crop of children. Her body must've been broken and her mind weary. We weren't poor, but we were a biscuit away from being on the street. I might not have remembered my parents' faces, but the welfare cheese and the large bag of fake cheerios stood out. My twin brother and I slept in dresser drawers, our sleeping quarters until our legs grew too long to fit anymore.

In the country, there was no school shopping. Grandma insisted we "jus' make do wit what we got." It was a two-mile walk to school through the woods. There was no such thing as bus transportation for children who went to Bethel Hill. It was a long way, but Grandma was going to walk with me and teach me everything I needed to know about the path.

Grandpa scared me out of my pants one day with a story about the coachwhip snakes that inhabited the same road I had to travel. As he told it, the legendary snakes were speedy and known to chase you down. They'd wrap their long bodies around you and whip you with their tails until you were dead. To make matters worse, they'd stick their tails up your nose to make sure you were no longer breathing. Grandma overheard Grandpa telling me about the snakes. She said, "Edgar, if you don' stop scarin' that chile with your ol' tales." She rolled her eyes and told me there was no such thing. She said men were sometimes known for their crazy ways and that I shouldn't pay Grandpa any mind.

When the first day of school came, we woke up early. Grandma and I had to leave the farm by six a.m. to cover the two miles to the fork in the road where Miss Clay, the teacher, would pick me up and take me the rest of the way. As we passed through the small wooden gate that separated our front yard from the road, Grandma told me not to be afraid. "God done cast you, chile, so you ain't got nothin' to fear." I wasn't sure exactly what that meant, but if Grandma said it, I knew it was true. When I told her how scared I was, all she said was, "Nobody want you but the dev'l and your ol' grandma, chile."

Up ahead of us, like a monolith sitting on a hill, was a massive pine tree. It became a fixture and pillar for me that marked where home was. I glanced back at it as I left and greeted it with relief on the way back. Grandma and I walked along with the woodlands on each side of us. Deep brush and weeds grew wild, lining the sides of the road. The sand was as white and grainy as table salt. It was quiet, with only birds chirping. We saw deer, snakes and glimpses of other creatures. Grandma showed me how the dirt road had no turns and would lead me straight to where I could look down into a small valley and see Cousin Jeff's house. This was to be an indication that I was almost at my destination, where I would wait for my ride. "Don' you worry yo'self chile, I be goin' with you all year." She never complained, despite her age.

After what seemed like forever, we got to the fork in the road. Grandma eased herself down onto a big rock. An old pale green Buick with peeling paint on the driver's side, stopped right in front of us. A woman sat in the driver's seat. She was rotund, had a jolly face and cat-eyed glasses resting on her nose. She leaned out the window and said, "Mornin' Miss Lula, hi you?"

"I'm a kickin' but not high, Miss Clay. Get on in, chile."

I crawled in trying not to look at her. I was afraid if I did, I'd burst into an endless round of tears. Miss Clay took off with a jerk. I turned around in my seat and caught a glimpse of Grandma with her walking stick, heading back toward home. That familiar sinking feeling of being left behind caught in the back of my throat.

The car sped away in a blaze of dust. The tires rattled as we passed over cattle crossings and cracks in the road. Miss Clay drove so fast I thought the engine was going to conk out. Suddenly, we screeched to a two-wheeled stop in front of Bethel Hill Elementary School. I tumbled out of the car. I didn't have much experience with other children since I left Detroit, but I knew right away I'd be forever branded as the teacher's pet, and worse. The other children stood around dressed in their new first-day-of-school clothes. All eyes were on me. They snickered and whispered to each other like only little kids do.

I must have looked a hot mess with my bare feet and no ribbons in my hair. I had small plaits all over my head that stuck out in all directions from the breeze of my wild ride. I wanted to shrink right then and there and dissolve into the sand. I thought about the bag of ribbons Miss Ruby Tarrt had given me. I tossed them so far under the house that I bet the chickens ate them. Grandma said they ate everything that wasn't nailed down. Those ribbons brought back painful memories of the last moment with my sister. It was that awful day when my world turned upside down and was cast into oblivion.

It was horrible thinking about my sister. Maybe I shouldn't have been so resistant when she tried to garnish my hair with those hideous things. To me, those ribbons symbolized ugliness. I was determined never to wear another ribbon in my hair, ever again. No matter how out of place I looked, I'd rather succumb to the ridicule of my classmates. That was my own personal protest and I was sticking to it.

Miss Clay waddled up to the schoolhouse door. There I stood, right where she dropped me, alone with thirty-five strangers' eyes on me. I illogically searched for my grandmother's face in the crowd. One of the boys rang a big bell that swung from a rope attached to a mulberry tree. Everyone took off running toward the school, laughing, giggling and shoving each other as they all jostled to get inside the door at the same time. I reluctantly trailed behind.

Bethel Hill Elementary was an old building with two classrooms and a closet in between. I was in the younger group with Miss Clay. Her enormous presence commanded the room. She must've weighed three hundred pounds. Her poor feet squishing out all around her shoes couldn't have been comfortable. She had a robust laugh and a front gold tooth that shone brightly when she smiled, which she did a lot.

The chitter-chatter of the children confused me; I was used to old people and old talk. As I looked around at how they dressed and interacted, I knew I didn't fit into that picture at all. My clothes looked like the pieces of cloth that Grandma used to patch her quilts; matter of fact, they were the same exact cloths. That meant I was wearing the clothes of dead people! I was a walking quilt.

The morning went by in a jumble of new impressions. At recess, I sat alone and miserable as the other children ran around screaming and playing. All the girls had pressed hair that was either neatly braided in three plaits or fixed in the three-pony-tail look, one on the top and one on each side. Grandma tried to press my hair with the hot comb once, but I ran away afraid of that scorching, smoking thing. I had no one but myself to blame for going to school nappy-headed, barefooted and miserable.

I spent the rest of the day in a self-conscious fog. When I came home I asked Grandma to press my hair. She didn't say a word, but there was a twinkle in her eyes as she heated up the comb. It slid through my hair making crackly sounds like when fireworks go off. I loved every minute of it. Grandma proclaimed that my hair was now "straight as an arrow, nigh go get them ribbons that Miss Ruby give you." I lied and told Grandma that I had made a mistake and dropped them down the outhouse stool while sitting there taking care of my business. She rose up, shook her head, and said "Chile, what I'm gonna do with you? You somethin' else."

The next day, I went to school with pressed hair and three pony-tails held together with rubber bands. I was still an eyesore. My classmates dressed better than me. They ate better than me, too. For lunch, they brought Vienna sausages or potted meat packed in a new brown paper bag every day. My lunches consisted of cold biscuits with mystery meat in a stained old paper bag. Grandma made sure I brought that same bag home every day no matter how many grease stains it had on it. I got teased about my lunch bags. I got ridiculed for living way out in the country, for being poor, and for looking like a scarecrow. Some of these classmates were actually my cousins, which didn't mean a hill of beans because they ridiculed me too. I was awkward and unhappy; it seemed like all my good qualities vanished.

I was left-handed, and for some reason, back in the 50's and 60's writing with your left hand was taboo and considered wrong. I insisted on having nothing to do with my right hand. I was what you would called a 'true lefty' until Miss Clay demanded that I'd be relegated to using my right hand for writing. She didn't care what other tasks were done with my left hand, but writing wasn't one of them. To insure I heeded to her edict, she'd pop me on my knuckles.

She had a paddle she called the "board of education." It had small circular holes in the fat part of it so when it hit your skin the holes became suction cups and sucked your skin up. It hurt like hell. I feared the "board of education" more than Grandma's "switch." She'd keep it in the corner of the classroom and no matter where you sat in that room, it was always in plain sight. This board became a huge deterrent to misbehavior during my years at Bethel Hill. Miss Clay's tactics eventually worked.

That first year in school, I desperately sought some sort of identity. I thought I was the only child at Bethel Hill, and maybe in the whole town of Livingston, who wasn't living with their parents. As the days passed and I began to make friends, I realized I wasn't the only child at Bethel Hill who was being raised by their grandparents. I spent many days sitting under the old mulberry tree during recess talking with my friend Rhoda. We ate homemade pecan candy that her grandmother made for her every Friday. Along with finally feeling like I fit in, I discovered I liked learning in class.

Miss Clay gave us an unusual education. Bethel Hill had terrible old worn-out textbooks, which was typical for most Black schools. "Fun with Dick and Jane" books were outdated. As an inquisitive child, I often commented on how no one in those books looked like me and my classmates. The weekly readers we had were worse than Dick and Jane. Miss Clay and the other teacher, Mrs. Shy, began bringing in the World Book and Britannica Encyclopedias and taught us directly from them, simplifying the material for our grade level. We went through those books from A to Z. Not only did we learn math, we also learned its origin. We got a broad and deep education, far better than any standard schoolbook. The school board never knew Miss Clay and Mrs. Shy weren't teaching us from the "approved" curriculum. Each time we received visits from the school superintendent, old Mr. Summers, Miss Clay and Miss Shy hid the encyclopedias in the cloakroom until he left.

I was a sponge, quickly absorbing everything. Miss Clay would ask, "Who can repeat this?" My hand shot up like a bullet every time. I volunteered reciting poems because I could memorize easily. I attributed this to Grandma's stories imbedding in my brain. I got straight A's. That was another thing that felt good. After a while, kids stopped ridiculing me. There was still occasional snickering about not having electricity and running water, but I was finally being accepted.

One day, Grandma told me my mother was coming to visit. I was shocked. I racked my brain trying to remember her face, but I couldn't. Thinking about seeing my mother made my heart pound. At that point, she was a stranger to me. Two days later, she was standing on our front porch.

When the car pulled up, I hid under the bed with my quilt wrapped around me like a cocoon, refusing to come out. When Grandma finally coaxed me out, hot tears steamed my face. My mother smiled at me, which made me cry even more. Grandma looked irritated, shaking her head at me, then went off with my mother to sit in the rockers and talk for hours.

The whole time my mother was there, I tried to avoid her. I had to be polite because Grandma wouldn't have it any other way, but other than that, I wouldn't say a word. The only thing I remember about that visit was my mother smiled without showing her teeth. No one ever told me why she was there. I was terrified she was going to take me away from Grandma Lula. Then, like an east wind on a summer day, she was gone. And I was still there- with Grandma in the kitchen, like every other day.

CHAPTER 6

BORN TO QUILT

Grandma said it was time to finish the story about Ella. I rushed out into the front yard to help her set up the quilting horse, eager to hear the rest of the story. When she settled in, she looked at me to make sure I was paying attention. She said the first thing I needed to understand was that Emma was a proud and strong woman. One of her greatest strengths was making quilts.

Maybe that didn't sound so special, but I should think about it: being a slave, but having the spirit to make something of her own creation. I was struck with the gravity of all the ugliness that invaded her environment. Through it all, she continued to brighten people's lives with her quilts. She injected light into the middle of all that darkness by stitching pieces of cloth together. Grandma claimed their Mama, Emma was born to make quilts.

"From the time I was jus' a li'l bitty chile I always watch. And b'fore me, she teach Ella to quilt. The quilts they make was some kinda special, not like ev'rybody else: they zigged and zagged and crissed and crossed, with lots and lots of colors. You can bet those folk up in the big house got themselfs some. They like showin' them off to the guests. Anybody can see they special. Well, sure 'nough, soon all them other White folk wants quilts fo' they self. Purty soon, Mama and Ella makin' quilts fo' White folk, lots and lots of quilts. They have a nice li'l bizness goin'. 'Magine that back in those days? Fac', Mama makin' a quilt for Ella when she was born, but she born early, so Mama nev'r finish it." She pointed to my quilt. I was stunned to realize that the quilt I loved so much was part of Ella's birth quilt. Grandma sighed. She told me how she adored her sister. The two of them went everywhere together. She copied Ella's behavior. How they must have been a sight! Tall Ella and little Lula.

"One day, trouble come in through the side door. The Young's give Ella some chil'ren's books they didn' want no more. Ella hear young Mr. Young jokin' that li'l nigga gal gone jus' look at them pictures, she nev'r gone learn to read noways. Hoo, boy, that set Ella off all right. Sure as night follow day, with Missus Young helpin' out, Ella got herself to readin' and right fas', too. The more she read, the smarter she get. She start teachin' all the Colored help how to read and write they names. There was some kind of uproar up there, let me tell you." Grandma laughed.

"Next thing you know, Ella got me to readin' too and talkin' proper like, almos' like White folk. We sit up half the night with jus' the moonlight, learnin' the bible. She jus' like a teacher, makin' sure I say the word right. Even though my sistah was born right after slav'ry, she sure did know a lot 'bout words. That's why I can look at the words in your schoolbook and make out what they say. I make sure I listen to ev'rythin' Ella say.

Mama tell Ella 'bout gettin' uppity, but Ella didn' pay no mind. She proud and don' listen to nobody. She ain't live through slav'ry times. Mama start worryin' somethin' fierce 'bout her oldes' daughter. Then the wurs' thing happen. Ella fall in love with a boy ov'r at the old Deaver Plantation. She fall head ov'r heels 'bout that boy; she walk 'round in a daze. His name was Jeremiah Deavers."

Grandma told me how the two "young-uns" spent the summer together "moonin' 'round," until Jeremiah's family decided to move to New York. Ella and Jeremiah were broken up about that, but Jeremiah promised to come back. He'd go to school, get a job, then come back and marry Ella and take her up north with him. They promised their hearts to each other.

"Jeremiah write all the time. Mama, Papa and me sit 'round the fire at night while Ella read his letters. We so proud of that boy. He up north and gettin' good book learnin'. I see it in Ella's eyes she so wants fo' that boy to come back fo' her. 'Twas a long three years, but Jeremiah come back, jus' like he say. He finish his schoolin' and got hisself a decent, good payin' job. Ella so happy to see him she near lif' off the ground. There wont one question that he the man fo' her; Mama and Papa saw it clear, and give her their blessin'. Jeremiah offer to bring Mama and Papa and me with them, but there no way Papa gone leave. Ella gone have to go all by herself." Heaviness descended over Grandma. She went on to say how Ella went up to the big house to tell the young Mr. Young that she was getting married and leaving them. She knew he wouldn't be happy about it, not at all.

"He was sittin' there in his study with a glass of whiskey. Ella gone stand 'cross from him in his ol' leather chair where she make him all them 'lixirs and plasters. When he look at her with them dev'lish eyes of his, she was scareder than a run'way slave. She know comin' to tell him wont gone be good. He wont nev'r let her go. It be ov'r his dead body. What else she gone do? She has to go with her Jeremiah. She gone have to tell young Mr. Young she gone get marry and goin' up north. He gets no more herbs, ain't makin' him no more quilts. She not gone be his good luck piece no more."

Grandma said she wished she'd seen Ella standing there defiant and unwilling to back down from the young Mr. Young. Years later when Grandma visited Mrs. Young at the Young plantation, she told Grandma what happened that night, saying how she witnessed the whole thing. Mrs. Young wanted to make sure Grandma knew the details of what occurred that night in the big house.

Grandma said, "Ella act like she didn' feel that slap 'cross her face 'cause she jus' stand there. Then the blood come runnin' out. Missus Young say Ella jus' starin' the young Mr. Young down, not movin' nary bit. She musta feel that blood runnin' down her face 'cause she touch her face like she tryin' to wipe 'way the blood. He stand there lookin' eye to eye at Ella. I know my Ella, she still ain't gone back down. I know this make him madder than a wet hen. Ella standin' there bleedin' to death, she tryin' to reason with young Mr. Young. Ev'ry time she talk, he knock her down again. This time with his fis'.'"

"Missus Young say Ella sound like she chokin' on her blood. He stand there and beat my Ella somethin' fierce, but she jus' kep' gettin' up and he get madder and madder. She lookin' him square dead in the eye. She was fix on lettin' him know that she leavin' and wont comin' back. I guess he figure he need to do somethin' to shut Ella up fo' good. That's when he take that hot poker and swing it. He set a right smart mark on the side of Ella's face and lip. Burnin' heat from that poker mess my Ella up so she could hardly open her mouth. He seal her mouth shut like brandin' a cow. Ella jus' crawl her way out the house onto the porch screamin' out fo' the Lord. Heaven only know how she make it back to the house that night."

"Ella's face so bad off. Lord know she in a lot of pain. Nobody, not even Satan hisself should suffer like that. I can only think how much pain my sistah in that night. My mama and papa was screamin' and a cryin'. We all in there hollerin', Papa ramblin' through the house lookin' fo' his huntin' rifle, he goin' after young Mr. Young. Mama goin' on and on, grabbin' Papa by the arm. 'No Joe, he gone kill you sure is I'm standin' here'."

"Papa pull 'way from Mama so hard she felt on the floor. She grab his legs, cryin' and screamin', tryin' to stop Papa from runnin' off killin' that White man. I ain't nev'r in my life seen Papa cry. But that night, it was all I can do to help Mama grab a holt of him and not let him go. I seen it in his eyes, so much hate, but he couldn' do nothin' but holt on to it. Papa lef'. He jus' disappear in the night and I nev'r see him again."

"Ella wont let Jeremiah nowheres near her. My sistah beg and plead with me to not let him see her like this. Her face was jus' too scarred. That boy's spirit jus' up and die that night. He lit on outta there like a bat outta hell. Jeremiah end up movin' back to the li'l plot of land that him and his family live b'fore they goes up north. He not able to see his Ella. I s'pose that boy jus' lost his mind."

Grandma said that young Mr. Young destroyed her entire family in one night. "Mama's heart mus' of broke so deep, she go to sleep that night and nev'r wake up. I was a young gal, jus' fo'teen years ol'. Po Ella bein' so bad off, Papa and Mama leavin' me like that, and Jeremiah... well that jus' more than a body could bear. But I have to bear it. I the only one lef'."

Things got worse. The next day, the young Mr. Young ordered them to "get on their way." He was taking back his land. With the help of Ella's church family, Grandma Lula said she buried Emma, and then left with Ella. They were taken in by some of the church folks at Pilgrim Home Baptist church, which was the church Emma belonged to.

Ella's mouth wouldn't completely heal. She could barely open it, making it difficult to eat. Grandma said she did the best she could caring for Ella, but her burns were just too severe. "Ella get so po' from not eatin', she jus' waste 'way. She didn' live long after that." The courageous Ella, both blessed and cursed, who had once found such joy in life, passed from this earth clutching Grandma's hand. Even as death took her, she faced it straight on.

"I wish I know where my sistah veil went to. She wear it day and night, even when she sleep. That's why I knows she have it 'round her neck that night she goes to young Mr. Young's place. That sorry sap prob'ly snatch it off her neck when he commence to beatin' on Ella. I was gone try to find it so I can send off my sistah right nice in her goin' to glory clothes. Only Lord know where it's at. I jus' didn' have no time to worry 'bout it then 'cause I have to put my sistah in the ground."

"I use to go up and visit Jeremiah ov'r yonder at the Deaver place jus' to check on him, make sure he alright. He wont the same boy no more. He hardly make 'nough from the li'l farmin' he was doin' to keep that place up. I sit with him fo' a spell, but he nev'r lif' up his head the whole time. He jus' kep' lookin' at the floor mumblin somethin' I pert'near couldn' make out. I didn' have the heart to tell that boy Ella was gone. He prob'ly wont understand no way."

"One day I gone to see him but he nowheres to be found. I make my way back down the road pass Ma Cherry's house. She outside swee-pin' the front porch and say, 'Come ov'r heah gal'. If you come by heah to see dat Deaver boy, he done gone on to glory. Dey find him hangin' from a tree down in the bottom. Didn' have a stitch of clothes on him'."

"I don' know what make me go back to Jeremiah's shanty and grab that ol' blue shirt of his. I 'spect it was a way to keep him and Ella to-gether. Now I got his shirt and Ella's white weddin' dress. The two fit together like hand in glove." I watched as Grandma searched the bag of rags until she found the blue shirt that belonged to Jeremiah. She put it next to the pieces of Ella's wedding dress. "You see chile, trouble don' las' always." As was customary when Grandma attempted to hide her sadness, she took the bottom part of her apron and wiped her face. The sweat seemed to camouflage her tears of sadness.

CHAPTER 7

MISS SUGAR AND AUNT HONEY BEE

Grandma had close relationships with so many people I could barely keep up with who was who. People came and went a lot. I'd look up and see folks coming down the road with their walking sticks. Sometimes they looked disheveled like they'd walked for miles. People loved Grandma Lula. Not only was she the best quilt maker around, she was the best peanut brittle and homemade cake maker too. Her fruitcakes were so popular, people placed their orders two years in advance. I often heard the old folks say that Grandma's fruitcake "could make a blind man see." I was dying to know the story behind such a fruitcake that had the power to give sight back to the blind. It wasn't long before I found out.

I learned that not only did Grandma keep homemade edibles in her locked chifferobe, she also stored what she called her bottle of "spirits" in there. She used these spirits in her fruitcakes. "Spirits" was a fancy way of saying alcohol and not the kind you put on your aches and pains. I guess that was why after people ate up her cakes, they left giddy and as light as feathers.

I started helping Grandma make her fruitcakes. She'd pull out her bottle of spirits and add a few cups to the batter. We'd pour the mix into twelve-inch pans and bake them in the oven for what felt like forever. Right before a crust formed on the top of the cake, we'd pull them out. Once they cooled, we'd place them in cake tins and off they went to sit under Grandma's bed for a year. Two days before Christmas, we'd fetch them from the dark abyss when the time was ripe for them to be devoured. The first time the top was removed, my oh my, the smell of spirits mixed in with the fruit and nuts nearly knocked me over.

One time, curiosity got the best of me and I wanted to know what made them so special. Grandma was in the fields so I decided to sneak in for a taste of my own. I crawled under the bed and searched the dark. Without much effort, I dragged out the first one I laid my hands on. When I opened the top, sure enough, the smell sent my senses into ecstasy. I was drooling like a pig as I sank my teeth into the first bite. I thought I'd died and went to heaven! I ate almost a fourth of that one fruitcake and probably would've downed the entire thing if I hadn't heard Grandpa approaching from the rear of the house. I closed the lid and shoved the remainder back under the bed as fast as I could.

All of a sudden, I was moving in slow motion. My head spun like a spinning top and I started giggling and slobbering all over myself. Grandpa saw me in the hallway and looked at me cross-eyed as I shot pass him down the dogtrot. I didn't remember anything after that, but when I woke up, I was under the house with the chickens not having a clue as to how I got there. I heard Grandma screaming the hell out of my name. It hurt my head. I scrambled from under the house looking guilty as sin. Grandma asked, "What wrong with you chile? You look like you drunk." I didn't have the slightest idea what "drunk" meant so I smiled at her and went on my way. She didn't let on, but I was pretty sure she knew what I'd been up to.

I loved watching Grandma give out her fruitcakes. She was more thankful to give them to folks, than they were to receive them. She got a lot of joy from the act of giving. She gave away her cakes and never asked for a cent. People begged Grandma to take their money, but she refused. I'd even see folks try and sneak money into her apron pocket when she wasn't looking. She was the most generous human being I'd ever known. I asked her why she always gave stuff away. She looked at me with that warm beam of love coming out of her eyes and said, "Chile, you can nev'r pay me 'nough fo' a smile or gracious heart. Grandma want you to always remember that."

A lot of folks ended up in our front yard to watch Grandma stitch quilts and listen to her stories. A common trait among the women who came was that they all had strong personalities. One of her oldest friends, and a regular guest, was Miss Sugar. Grandma met Miss Sugar right after she married Grandpa Edgar. She didn't know Miss Sugar's parents, but something told me she wished she had so she could see who created this wild child.

Of all the women who came to our house in the woods, Miss Sugar was the most animated of them all. She'd pull up in a yellow and white Buick Electra 225, "a deuce and a quarter." That thing was a sight! Long and sleek and looked like it stretched from one end of our front yard to the other. Miss Sugar wore loud colored dresses with hats to match. She was statuesque, looking like she came straight out of a fashion magazine. She wore gobs of makeup in blood-red shades and her dimples were so deep I could fit my entire body in them. She had a booming voice and a voracious laugh that could be heard for miles.

Grandma was about ten years older than Miss Sugar, but they were best friends. I couldn't help but wonder what made them blend. One thing Grandma didn't like was when Miss Sugar sang the blues. She said it was the "Dev'ls" music. Miss Sugar loved the blues. She sang so well it was easy to overlook how risqué some of the lyrics were. Sometimes Miss Sugar put on a concert right there in our front yard. She came with what folks down south called "The dirty, stankin' blues." One of the songs she sang was about a man who went down to the juke joint and caught his wife with the piano player:

"My li'l gal den went to the hootchie coochie joint
Slippin' and slidin', with the piano man
Ran to de front door, he ran out de back
Got my li'l gal wit him and das a fact
Ooooh, hootchie, coochie, ooooh hootchie coochie."

Miss Sugar would jump and dance all over the front yard. She'd wave her dress around like a fan. Every fly, bug and mosquito that was anywhere near her, ran for shelter so they wouldn't get caught in the hem of her dress. Grandma told Miss Sugar that she needed the Lord. Miss Sugar said, "No, what I need is a good, strong man, Miss Lula." Miss Sugar would've made a helluva comedian. Even Grandpa skinned and grinned when Miss Sugar came around. His old bones moved faster than I'd ever seen trying to get out to the front yard just to see her. Grandma would burst out, "Edgar, I thought you was down in your legs this evenin'. You movin' kinda quick now, don' hurt yo'self."

Miss Sugar's husband, Mr. Tank, was the total opposite of her. He was a quiet man who jumped at her command. When he came with her on those visits to the country, she'd say, "Tank do this, Tank pick up that, Tank go here, Tank go there, Tank don't do that." That poor man didn't know whether he was coming or going. He just did what he was told.

I think Mr. Tank would wallow in a pile of mess if Miss Sugar told him to.

Miss Sugar and Mr. Tank lived up on the north side of Livingston in a small town called Bellamy. They had running water and an indoor toilet. Miss Sugar would proudly announce that their house was 'built from the ground up' by Mr. Tank and his brothers. She said she refused to marry Mr. Tank unless he could build her a brick house with electricity. I heard her say to Grandma how Mr. Tank could give her the world, but couldn't give her a baby.

He was a little man, not much taller than I was. I felt sorry for him. Grandma tried playing mediator between the two. After hearing too much of Miss Sugar giving orders, she'd finally say, "Now let that man be, Sugar." Mr. Tank was the nicest man I ever met, always smiling. There wasn't one time he didn't come down to the country and bring me a bag of peppermint candy canes. He must've loved Miss Sugar to no end. Why else would he put up with her mess?

Miss Sugar had a bunch of money. She had her own butter, milk and cream business. Folks said she started out with just a couple of cows and two old churns. Grandma said Miss Sugar would sit on her back porch and churn until her hands were raw, then hitch up two mules and go to town selling her milk and butter. I couldn't imagine Miss Sugar doing this every day because churning butter is hard work.

I remembered the day Grandma first taught me how to churn. I was playing down by the creek when I heard Grandma call my name. It was so loud and in such a way, I'd swear up and down I was in serious trouble. When I reached the back porch, I was out of breath and probably looked as guilty as sin. Grandma was sitting on one of her old tree trunks that probably weighed a thousand pounds. For the life of me, I couldn't imagine how they moved those stumps onto the enclosed back porch. Grandma sat there perched, her dress pulled back with a tall brown bowl-shaped contraption sitting between her legs. It had a long skinny stick that fit into a small round hole that was attached to the wooden platform. Grandma sat grasping the stick with both hands. "Come on chile, Grandma gonna teach you how to make butter." She began pushing the stick up and down like a plunger, singing away.

Come butter come
Butter gone come
Come butter come

She was sweating from ear to ear. The red and white headscarf she was wearing was soaking wet as she leaned against the stick, resting and out of breath. When she pulled back the wooden platform from the large container, I looked inside expecting to see some magical thing happen, but was disappointed to find only a few butter curdles had risen to the top. "Come on now, we gotta get some more butter to rise," she said as I placed my bottom on the makeshift chair while Grandma guided my hands in just the right way.

Off I went, singing that same butter song that she was singing and sweating just as hard. I churned until my hands felt like all the skin fell off. I couldn't muster up enough energy to manage one more second of butter making until Grandma removed the lid to discover a huge band of butter. "Chile, you done make a whole heap of butter." I watched as Grandma took a wooden spatula and gently removed what had coagulated on top of the milk. I felt so good that my energy and confidence boosted me into a second wind. I ended up helping Grandma make a heap of butter that day. It was hard to imagine Miss Sugar doing that every day. My hands ached just thinking about it. She deserved all the accolades in the world for turning two cows and a couple of churns into a milk and butter empire, especially for a Black woman.

Grandma made me go play while they sat and talked. Miss Sugar would say, "Come here li'l nigger. You can come and sit on Miss Sugar's lap as long as you want," then turn to Grandma and say, "Please, Miss Lula, let that skinny li'l gal sit here. We ain't gonna talk about shit anyway, jus' tell a few lies, that's all Miss Lula." She'd laugh so hard that we laughed right along with her. Grandma told me Miss Sugar was known for smoking the wacky weed that "growed wild down below

Conkuby Creek." She said she smoked the weed for her headaches. I heard Grandma tell Grandpa, "You got to sometimes take what Miss Sugar say with a grain of salt." I had no idea what that meant.

Although Miss Sugar made a grand entrance when she arrived, her departure was as equally dramatic. She'd say, "I got to sing ya'll a song 'fore I leave. 'Spose I get out there and come to my death, so I got to leave ya'll with somethin', jus' in case." She'd break into one of those old bluesy numbers as she sashayed to her car, put on her sunglasses and take off down the road. The music blared as her hat bobbed to and fro in the breeze.

Another good friend of Grandma's was Honey Bee. She was the daughter of my great- grandma Alice's sister. Most Blacks didn't care for Aunt Honey Bee because she was what folks down south called "selective White" or "selective Black." This meant that Aunt Honey Bee acted White when she needed to, and then slip into what Miss Sugar called her "nigger routine," when she was around Black folks. Miss Sugar and Aunt Honey Bee had a couple of ugly run-ins. It was widely known they didn't like each other. Grandma never said why and I was never able to pick up on the reason during one of my eavesdropping sessions.

Aunt Honey Bee's hair was long and flaming red. Her skin was pure white, sprinkled with freckles. I'd swear on my own life that she was a White lady had I not been told otherwise. Folks called her "Apron Lady" because she made the most elegant aprons you'd ever seen. Her aprons were almost as famous as Grandma's quilts. Even though her husband left her a nice dowry, she pulled in a decent income from her apron sales.

In the south, the apron was a garment that every God-fearing, decent, older woman had to have. Aunt Honey Bee wore hers with a glowing pride. These weren't just little aprons you'd throw around your waist. They covered your entire chest. Above all else, they had two big pockets to put your wares in. They came in all types of colors and designs; some with ruffles, some with bursts of flowers and some printed with all types of fruits and vegetables.

Aunt Honey Bee was born on the other side of Livingston. She had a brother and sister who remained there, but she went to Detroit when she was twenty years old. While in Detroit, she passed as a White woman. During her time there, she cut ties with her family in order to keep her racial identity a secret. She married a White man and told him she had no family so he wouldn't find out her real ethnicity. Aunt Honey Bee was "passing." This occurred when light skinned Blacks passed as White in order to get ahead in the world.

Aunt Honey Bee's husband desperately wanted children. She was afraid that genetics would betray her, so she used herbs to keep from getting pregnant. Whatever she was taking eventually made her barren and she never did have any children. Her husband was from old money and owned a slew of textile businesses. When he died, she sold the company to his family and came back to live in Livingston. Her relationship with her family was fragile for the rest of the time Aunt Honey Bee remained on this earth. Her sister and brother never forgave her for hiding her roots. They lived only a few miles from her, but never visited.

Grandma was one of very few Blacks who didn't have a problem with Aunt Honey Bee. As far as she was concerned, Aunt Honey Bee was a part of her family and she would love her through all of her faults. Whenever I saw her, she'd give me a big hug and asked the same question each time: "Are you minding your Grandma?" She always wanted to see my report card and doted on me when I got straight A's. Grandma would have me stand up and repeat the 27th Psalm and the 121st Psalm, which I memorized in school. When I was done, Grandma and Aunt Honey Bee gave me a standing ovation. Aunt Honey Bee pumped up my little head every time I saw her. She was self-assured and well educated. When words rolled off her lips, you'd hear every last syllable. She had style and grace and a proper way about her that I liked.

G randpa's sister, Great Aunt Bessie, was another regular visitor. She was a piece of work. She was the most outspoken woman I ever met. For a woman to be this brazen was a rarity. One day, I overheard Grandpa tell her "Ya know Bessie, dat's why you can't keep no husband. You jus' too damn orn'ry. What man gonna put up wit your shit?"

Nobody knew how many times Bessie was actually married, but she had two husbands who mysteriously died. She was six feet tall, mean as a snake, and had braids on each side of her head that came down to her waist. Like Grandpa, she carried every bit of her "hushed bloodline" trait.

Most people who lived in and around Livingston knew Bessie Horn and her strange idiosyncrasies, but she was what I called "country elegant." She had a certain flair and arrogance about her. The first time I laid eyes on her, she was moving like a swirling tornado rushing in to wipe out everything in its path. Her stockings hung down on her legs because they lost all their elasticity. Her shoes looked like she'd had them since the turn of the century.

She had an apron for every day of the week. Since she visited almost daily, I knew which day of the week it was because of what apron she had on. She never switched up days. On Monday's, she wore a blue and white plaid one with ruffles that ran around the edge of the bib and sashes. That apron looked too dainty and didn't fit with Aunt Bessie's surly personality. My favorite one was her Friday apron. It had squirrels, raccoons and walnuts printed around the entire width.

I heard Grandpa talking to Grandma about how Aunt Bessie had an inside pocket in each of those aprons where she'd keep her bankroll of money. In the left pocket, she carried a 32 pistol, which wasn't hard to see when she plopped down in the straw bottom chair in the front yard. The front butt of her gun would protrude from her apron pocket.

Aunt Bessie didn't trust banks and was afraid that since she toted her money around, someone would try to steal it from her. She was known to give out loans to family and friends and would charge interest when they returned the money, just like a bank. This was how she acquired extra land from borrowers. They'd put up their land as collateral. When the money wasn't paid on time, Aunt Bessie took their land right out from under them. I heard she didn't even give one-day grace period on her loans. Like I said, mean as a snake.

I wondered if some business deal went sour between Aunt Honey Bee and Aunt Bessie. The animosity between those two was palpable. If I had to guess, it probably had to do with those beautiful aprons Aunt Bessie wore. They had Aunt Honey Bee's signature all over them. Her aprons were unique. Every apron that Aunt Honey Bee wore had a thick, crooked stitch in the shape of a bee in all four corners of the bib. Just like Grandma's quilts, you could always tell her brand by their style and pattern.

One day Grandma and Aunt Bessie were sitting under the big oak tree when along came Miss Sugar in her Electra 225. She pulled up right in the front yard. Before long, Aunt Honey Bee drove up in her custom-made Impala, which was just as sleek as Miss Sugar's car. These two women were alike in many ways. They both indulged in the finer things in life and dressed like they were going to the opera. Aunt

Honey Bee was sure enough a showstopper. I think Miss Sugar didn't like being upstaged by Aunt Honey Bee, and vice-versa. One thing for sure, it was darn entertaining watching the two of them vie to be the center of attention.

Sometimes I'd crawl from the back yard to the front through the underbelly of the house where the chicken laid their eggs. That allowed me to see without anyone knowing I was there. That dark refuge became a place where I listened to grown folks talk about all the goingons. "This heres grown folk talk. It ain't for a chile's ears," Grandma would say.

It wasn't the most desirable place in which to eavesdrop, but sacrifices had to be made if I wanted to get in on the hottest gossip in the county. After all, me and those chickens were now in accord. Not like it was when I first got there.

The older I got, the more my ears burned to hear the stuff spewing from the lips of those who gathered in our yard. There wasn't much else to do living in the country besides try and find out how much mischief I could get myself into. Unlike Detroit, there were no neighborhood children to play with unless I traveled a couple of miles down the road.

I'd lay there for hours with my hands planted on each cheek, elbows firmly in the dirt. Miss Sugar, Aunt Honey Bee and Aunt Bessie provided the most spirited conversations. When Grandma "shooed" me away to go and complete my chores while grown folks talked, I already knew where I'd set up shop. I looked forward to it. The only thing missing was some of Grandma's teacakes.

As the four of them sat there, Grandma was doing all the talking, Miss Sugar was doing all the eye rolling, Aunt Bessie was sucking her teeth, and Aunt Honey Bee just sat there listening "cool as a cucumber," as Grandma would say. Then Miss Sugar opened her big ass mouth and said, "So, Honey, your brother got nothin' to do wit' you since you wanna act White?" Aunt Bessie followed suit with "Yeah, I heard 'bout that." Aunt Honey Bee started throwing big words out at both of them. I swear Aunt Bessie and Miss Sugar's heads spun around twice. Aunt Honey Bee spoke without raising her voice. With her legs crossed all lady-like, she didn't frown or flick one curse word back

It must've worked because after the last word came out of Aunt Honey Bee's mouth, there was nothing but silence. Aunt Bessie got up to leave and said, "Well, Miss Lula, you go on wit' your comp'ny." Miss Sugar almost knocked Bessie over when she decided to leave too. She said, "Well, Miss Lula, I ain't gonna sit 'round here and listen to this nigger cuss me out," even though Aunt Honey Bee didn't spit out one single harsh word. That was my first experience in learning that you don't have to raise your voice to get your point across. I knew from that day forward I wanted to learn the big words that Aunt Honey Bee was using. The words came off her tongue as crisp as the sheets I took off the clothesline.

I didn't want Grandma to find out I was eavesdropping on adult conversation. She started calling me in her usual booming voice that could wake the dead. I made my way from under the house covered in bird shit and smelling like it too. I shook off the crap and planted one of those 'I'm bored-as-hell' looks on my face as I started pulling the sheets and clothes off the line before she made it to the backyard. The way she looked at me, I got the feeling that deep down she knew I'd been lurking around somewhere listening in. She never said anything about it, but I knew she knew.

CHAPTER 8
THE GIFT THAT WASN'T

Since Bethel Hill Elementary School was so rural, we were easily forgotten by the education system. It was way out on a dirt road across from an old Black community called the *Moore Place*. There was a run-down juke joint sitting in an open field near the mulberry tree in our play area. The building was falling apart. Our schoolbooks were pitiful, and we didn't have enough of them. We didn't have enough supplies of any kind. I imagined how hard it must've been for Miss Clay. She took her job seriously and was a good teacher. I adored her to no end.

When the second year of school came around, I just turned six. Grandma said I was ready to make the walk to school on my own. She gave me her favorite walking stick to act as my "rod and staff." It towered way over my head and probably weighed as much as me. Grandma would say, "There ain't nothin' like a good walkin' stick." It had multiple uses, from beating snakes, to lifting laundry from the cooking pot, to shooing away stray dogs. I carried it back and forth every day.

Miss Clay was my hero. She made the best of what little she had. The math books we had were old and dilapidated, so she wrote her own math problems and used an old mimeograph machine that was donated by the Black high school to reproduce them. As sure as clockwork, the first Monday of every month, she'd hand out math problems and we'd sit in class working them out. She had us write book reports or make oral presentations from our studies of the encyclopedias. Sometimes she'd give us a topic and other times, she let us find our own that were interesting to us. I always chose the oral presentation because I had turned into a ham.

Miss Clay said I was a "born orator." I recited poems and sang. Grandma taught me so many poems and spirituals I had an entire arsenal at my disposal. Miss Clay would sit at her desk grinning and stomping her feet while the children clapped and chimed in. By the time I'd hit the chorus line, Bethel Hill was rocking. People passing by must've heard the hand clapping and desk-knocking thinking they were hearing the school band.

One day, Miss Clay excitedly announced we were getting new textbooks from the Alabama Board of Education. This was a day to rejoice. Both the students and teachers were thirsty for new material. Even though it was never talked about, our teachers wanted us to have the same educational opportunities as the White schools. A few days later, a White lady in a station wagon pulled up in front of the school. That station wagon gleamed and stood out amongst the dusty surroundings. The lady got out, smiling and greeted Miss Clay and Mrs. Shy. She went to the back of the station wagon, opened the door, and pointed to six cardboard boxes. Miss Clay called some of the older boys to lift them from the trunk of the car.

You would've thought Santa Claus had come to town- all us children jumping up and down. Mrs. Shy brought her kids from the next room. We sat in our chairs as the lady with the station wagon gave a speech about the textbooks. She said Negro children didn't get books of this quality, but she'd begged the school board for them. She claimed she had a special place in her heart for Coloreds. Miss Clay and Mrs. Shy rolled their eyes at each other, but kept their faces straight.

When the White woman finished her speech, Miss Clay brought the class to the front of the room. All in one voice, we recited the Pledge of Allegiance and sang "The Battle Hymn of The Republic" as Miss Clay, Mrs. Shy and the White lady stood there beaming with pride. We sang with so much fervor and conviction you'd of thought we were the Mormon Tabernacle Choir. We sang for all the times that Miss Clay told us that someday we'd receive good books and school supplies; we sang for all those hours that Miss Clay's brother spent fixing leaky ceilings and outhouses that overflowed. We sang for all those who'd come before us struggling on little or nothing from the Alabama Board of Education. We sang our hearts out.

The White lady said her goodbyes and God bless you's then she drove away. We stood on the steps of Bethel Hill School as she waved to us and took off down the long dirt road toward the highway. We couldn't wait to open those boxes and rushed back into the classroom where Miss Clay put one on the table. She made us step back. Then, as Mrs. Shy looked on expectantly, she cut the box open and lifted the lid. Both their faces froze.

I got a terrible feeling something was wrong. They opened another box – the same reaction; they both looked as though they'd been drained of blood. We were jumping up and down, dying to see our new books. They looked in the other boxes and without a word, closed them back up. Mrs. Shy secured the boxes with thick tape while Miss Clay sat there looking somber. Even her gold tooth no longer shimmered the way it usually did. Mrs. Shy cleared her throat and told all of us we were released for the day and we'd talk about the day's events tomorrow.

We were all confused. Nobody said a thing as we filed out the front door. I sat and waited on the front steps pouting. It hurt me to see Miss Clay so upset. She came out through the front door and looked at me with blank, tearful eyes. She walked right past me with her purse clutched against her chest. I ran alongside her, down the hill to her car. Something had changed her that day. She wasn't that same, effervescent woman I'd come to know and love. I longed to know what was in those boxes and why whatever was in them, made her so sad. We rode along in silence until she dropped me off at my regular spot. I watched her slowly drive off as a big question mark sat heavy on my head.

For years, those taped up boxes sat in our cloakroom. They became a part of the closet's décor. We used them as ladders to climb up on the top shelf to retrieve our hats and gloves. Everyone seemed to have forgotten about that day, never knowing what lay buried in the pit of those cardboard boxes. I was determined to learn the mystery behind them and wasn't going to let anything get in the way of finding out.

Living out in the country without a lot of things to occupy my mind, I tended to zoom in on a cause or a situation and refused to let go. I concocted a plan to walk the extra miles home without a ride from Miss Clay. I talked my friend Rhoda into joining me on the adventure. It was all we talked about for a week. The adrenaline and excitement of something forbidden drove our passion to new heights. I told Miss Clay I didn't need her to drop me off at my regular spot. She looked me over through her cat-eyed glasses as if something just wasn't quite right. I told her I'd be going to Rhoda's house for a spell. As she wobbled down the hill to her car sitting under the shade tree, we watched her drive away until we could no longer see the green from the back end of her car.

I went around the side of the building and climbed through the one window that never closed properly and shimmied myself inside. It was Rhoda's job to stay outside and keep watch. I tiptoed through the classroom and down the hallway to the cloak closet. All this sneaking around started to make me question whether or not this was a good idea. I ignored the thought and carefully pulled the tape off of one of the boxes and peered in.

In the darkness, I saw silhouettes of the dreaded Dick and Jane. As my eyes adjusted, I put my hand in and touched the cover of the book; it was another tattered hand-me-down from the White school. The books were more ragged than the ones sitting on the shelves of our classroom. We had received leftovers once again. It took a minute for the impact to sink in. As I closed the box, a bad feeling came over me. For the first time, I began to understand the magnitude of just how little we counted for in this world.

I climbed out the window and Rhoda immediately demanded to know what I found out. I tried to explain what I'd seen, stuttering and stammering, trying to make sense of it all. I told her everything in those boxes were old and tattered. She could tell by the look on my face, nothing more needed to be said. Rhoda and I never talked about that day again and our teachers never found out.

CHAPTER 9

COOTER

Fall blew in with a cool wind. I'd play in the leaves that swirled down and engulfed the yard. I'd rake them into piles and hide. When Grandpa ambled out into the front yard, he'd call out, "Where you at, Gal?" I'd bide my time, then pop up like a jack-in-the-box to surprise him. We'd stand there howling with laughter until Grandma appeared at the front door, "Stop all that noise! Y'all as crazy as chickens. C'mon, chile, run get me a cotton sack from the smokehouse. We burnin' daylight."

On Saturday mornings we got up bright and early to complete our chores. Since Grandma didn't do any plowing on this day, we had extra time. Even though it was Saturday, we still got up at six in the morning. Grandma said, "If the flower bloom, the rooster crow and the bird sang ev'ry single day at the same time. We ain't no dif'frent." We'd pull the quilting horse from the barn into the front yard and line it up just right so we'd be shielded from the sun by the oak tree.

One day, Grandma let me pick out the cloth to use in my quilt. I got all excited, thinking maybe I could break the run of death rags in my quilt and find something happier. Then I remembered all the cloths in Grandma's bag were from people who'd passed on. Oh, well. Without looking, I plunged my hand into the sack. I pulled out some colorful pieces. One was soft yellow and gray with small circles on it. It was the sleeve of a woman's dress, oddly shaped and needing to be cut. Grandma smiled when she saw it. She kept it, put it aside, and put the other pieces back. She searched through the bag until she found exactly what she was looking for: a bright orange material. It could have been a shirt or dress at one time, but now it was half torn with some buttons on it.

Grandma showed me how to cut it neatly into strips. She did the same with the yellow piece until we had six perfectly straight pieces. She placed two pieces of the yellow one, and three pieces of the orange one, next to Ella's wedding dress. She used straight pins to hold them in place until she could sew them together.

Grandma didn't start her story until she was sewing. It seemed like she had to be in the right state of mind before she could do justice to the stories she told. On that day, she began telling of the time she worked for Doc Rogers in Laurel, Mississippi. Her expression held something different than usual; there was a little wry smile on her face. I knew this story would be one to remember.

"When I work for Doc Rogers, I was all the time busy; wont time to do all the things I needs to do for a big house like his. I have to feed and nurse the chil'ren. I sew, cook meals, and I even take care of his ol' mama. So Doc Rogers hire a Colored woman to take in his laundry. Her name was Cooter Mae Berry. Cooter have four sistahs. She and the sistahs all work together gettin' out laundry. Cooter the only one of the sistahs that ev'r take a husband. She marry Jake Greenfield. He start out all right, but when his hand got caught up in that cotton gin, he couldn' get work nowheres. He turn into a no 'count drunk. He do nothin' all day, then come home drunk as a skunk and get to beatin' and wailin' 'way on Cooter. He beat her black and blue." Grandma shook her head and tsk'ed.

"Cooter put up with his mess 'cause they have four chil'ren, twin girls and two boys. She wont them chil'ren to have some kind of fam'ly.

She figure she can hold up fo' them. The twins name Jan and June, and the boys Thursday and Friday. She always askin' the Lord to make things better. Now, I'm here to tell ev'rybody who got ears to hear: laundress work is some back-breakin', soul-robbin' work you ev'r wanna see. Most folk think pickin' cotton or sharecroppin' is hard work, but a laundress job is some kinda hard and nobody know 'bout how bad. Folk today can't even think 'bout what them women have to go through. That work spoil many a laundress."

Grandma said these women picked up the laundry from their customers on Monday, which was due back to them on Wednesdays. On Wednesdays, they'd pick up clothes from their other customers. Wednesday's laundry was due back to those customers on Friday, so there wasn't room to breathe in between. The next week, it started all over again. The way Grandma described the washing assembly line that Cooter and her sisters had going on, was nothing short of amazing. The sisters had houses next to each other in the Black settlement. There were a bunch of clotheslines that hung from the first sister's house to the last sister's house.

Huge black iron pots were used for "cooking" the clothes. The water was scalding hot. They had to be careful transferring the clothes from the pot to the rinsing tub or their skin would bubble with burn marks. Grandma said, "One of the sistahs burnt half side her leg when the scaldin' water spilt on her. She got no choice but to keep on washin' and a-singin'. Singin' 'bout the Lord ease many folk pains, don' you forget that."

"They sep'rate them clothes, and heat the water 'til it boilin' in them big ol' black iron pots. Colored clothes, they toss down into them big ol' 'luminum tubs full of cool water. The white clothes, and the extra dirty ones, they throw them into the boilin' water so's to give 'em the extra loosenin' up. After they boil, they pull 'em out with they walkin' sticks, toss 'em in the cool water, then wring 'em out with they bare hands and hang 'em on the line for dryin'."

Cooter and her sisters made their own soap from Devil Lye. The lye was a dangerous chemical; I knew this because Grandma made her own soap with it. It came in a white can with red lettering and a skull and cross-bone. Grandma said the crystals would burn a hole in you if it came in contact with your skin. I'd cry when she asked me to bring it to her. How could you scare the shit out of a little girl with that talk and in the next breath, ask her to go fetch it?

The laundresses made their own starch from flour, water and Lord knows what else. She said they could heavy starch a shirt so much it'd stand up on its own. Each piece of clothing had to be scrubbed clean as a whistle on a scrub board. Grandma got a kick out of describing how Cooter and her sisters scrubbed their clothes on their individual boards in perfect rhythm with each other. "They be all line up side by side. The sistahs have they own 'quipment. Big ol' hundred-gallon tubs, pots, and scrub boards, they all have they own part of the songs they sung. Them sistahs singin' and scrubbin', scrubbin' and singin'."

Steal away, steal away, steal away to Jesus
I ain't got long to stay here.

"Them songs was mostly 'bout pain and mis'ry, sangin' they hearts out. Them hands goin' up and down on them scrub boards swoosh, swoosh, swoosh. Sun up to sun down, come weekdays, all year long they be out there. All them songs of trouble come out that wash yard of Cooter and her sistahs. A slew of po' women that live in the Colored settlement took in laundry too. They songs mix in with Cooter and her sistahs. Wont jus' Cooter and her sistahs, chile. All them women have to make a livin' some kinda way. Hands be glidin' up and down those ol' wooden boards; lot of rheumatiz' and sores on the skin of those ol' Black hands ov'r the years."

I got as jumpy as a shirt full of ants when Grandma was describing this. The scene was familiar to me. We'd pass the settlement where Cooter and her sisters had once lived when I rode in the back of Cousin Jeff's truck on the way into town. Cooter Mae and her sisters were long gone, but a new set of women had taken their place. I'd hunker down in the back of the truck so only my eyes were peeking over the side and I caught glimpses of the present day laundresses.

There they were, washing and tussling with the clothes as we slowed down at the railroad track. These women were out there in torrid conditions sawing away on their scrub boards. It awed me to think how tired they must be. Sometimes I'd see one of them sitting under a shade tree fanning herself with one of the old church cardboard fans, the one with a picture of the White baby Jesus with a halo around his head. Her dress was pulled up above her knees trying to catch a blow before she'd go back, arm deep in the silver washtub.

I didn't chime in. I knew better than to interrupt one of Grandma's stories. She went on. "When it rain, the sistahs have to do a right smart dance to make up for los' time, seein' how some of they customers show no mercy 'cause of the weather. Sometime it even snow. On them days it take some doin' to get them clothes to them customers on time.

They have to drape the clothes all ov'r the house and build a roarin' fire jus' so the clothes dry. Thank God for them heatin' irons. They made out of heavy iron jus' like them irons yonder." Grandma pointed to the irons we kept near the fireplace. "The sistahs put them on top of the hot stove till they pipin' hot. They iron them clothes till they almos' dry. Sometime they up all night tryin' to get them clothes ready for them White folk. Some of them customers want 're-dos' at the drop of a dime jus' 'cause they feel like it. Them re-dos was a sore trial."

"Cooter and her sistahs deliv'r them baskets of clean clothes in a ol' wagon hitch to a mule. Carry them heavy baskets 'round to the back door, seein' how no laundress nev'r 'llowed to come to the front door. I feel real bad 'bout Cooter; she have a real rough row to hoe. When she get back home at the end of the day, dead-tired, she cook supper for her chil'ren and start prayin' that her husband wont come home. She jus' bone-weary and it get mighty hard to keep up with all that work, then she get beat real reg'lar. She get to where she nev'r smile no more. Cooter nev'r fuss or say a harsh word to nobody and she walk like an ol' woman, all bent ov'r b'fore her time."

"I worry for her; 'tween her laundry and her husband, she have one leg in the grave. Her sistahs worry for her, too, with that no-good Jake comin' in, lightin' into her, drivin' her down." Grandma said she knew they weren't going to put up with too much more of his mess.

"Sure 'nough, one night Jake come home, drunk as an old boar. He bang 'round the house, yellin' for Cooter and knockin' furniture 'round. Now, Cooter leave some baskets of fresh laundry in the front room, ready for 'livery the next day. Jake knock it all aside, scatterin' them clean clothes ev'rywhere, and spoilin' all her hard work. Then he bang into the bedroom and lit into Cooter. He wallop her like it was a reg'lar night. But what he didn' know was he done cross the line. He mess with her laundry."

"The next day, Jake sittin' 'round talkin' big to his other sorry no-'count men folk down at the juke joint, when up pop Cooter's four sistahs. Did I tell you these sistahs was some big-bone, strong women? All them years liftin' big heavy baskets of clothes? Cooter's sistah's tell me 'bout how ol' Jake look when he see the sistahs standin' ov'r him. The surprise on his face would done Cooter good to see, if only she could. My Lord."

Grandma described how the four sisters dragged Jake outside and gave him a brutal walloping. Jake didn't know what hit him. "They let him know they didn' like what he doin' to their sistah. Jus' for good measure, they show him '*xactly* what gone happen if he ev'r lay a finger on their sistah again. He sure 'nough got the message." Grandma said he disappeared from town that night and was never heard from again.

"After that beatin' they put on him, Cooter's spirits revive. She got that spring back in her step. She even start sangin' in the 'sembly line again. She work and save 'nough money to send all her chil'ren up north to college. All the sistahs was so glad to see Cooter heavin' them clothes 'round jus' like reg'lar."

Cooter's yellow and orange prints were arranged strategically throughout the outer edges and middle of my quilt, and some right next to Ella's dress. I know Cooter would've been pleased with the way Grandma wove her into that quilt. Grandma left me with a song that day. It was one of Cooter's favorites that she and her sisters often sang on their washdays. A song Grandma often sang when she came home from toiling in the fields.

Bringing in the sheaves
Bringing in the sheaves
Here we come rejoicing
Bringing in the sheaves...

CHAPTER 10
MISS'SSIPPI HEARTBREAK

O ne of the best things about visits from Aunt Bessie was that she had the scoop on all the gossip, and she would tell it all. Most of the relatives thought Aunt Bessie was the biggest troublemaker of all Grandpa Edgar's fifteen sisters and brothers. She earned this reputation because, as Grandpa said, "She stir shit up and keep it goin' from sunup to sundown and den some."

Usually Grandma frowned on having me around when "grown folk" were talking, but I figured since I was helping with the quilt, the rules would bend. Aunt Bessie was the ideal conversationalist because "whatever came up, came out." That was Bessie's motto. If you didn't like it, you were shit out of luck. Boy, could she cuss. Grandma detested cuss words. Most times, Aunt Bessie kept them in check around Grandma, but when she got alone with Grandpa, it was a different story. Around him, she'd let the cuss words fly.

She'd scoot up into Grandma's face so close she could see the hair in her nostrils; then she looked around and spoke in a low, secretive voice. That tickled me because the nearest person who could possibly hear what she was saying, lived over two miles down the road. She proceeded to rake over the goings-on around town. She was famous for her scuttlebutt about other folk's children. "Dat yalla gal got all dem boys chasin' after her, she need to keep her draws up and her dress down."

Aunt Bessie was a good one for labeling folks by color. I'd hear her say, "Ya know so and so's boy is black as tar," or "you know that yalla gal's pappy is White." And her favorite one was, "I felt like slappin' the black off dat boy." Not once did I ever hear Aunt Bessie call folks by their names unless she prefaced it with their skin color first. I often heard folks label Aunt Bessie as being "color struck." I could understand why.

Grandma picked through pieces of cloth from her bags of rags and pulled out a brand new red and white plaid. I was especially curious because usually, the cloths were old and worn. Grandma caressed her cheek with it. Aunt Bessie gave her a sideways glance with those know-it-all eyes and said, "Miss Lula, you still think 'bout dat li'l White gal don'cha?" Grandma got a far off lonely look in her eyes and tears began welling up. We all got silent. Even Aunt Bessie was at a loss for words. Grandma picked up her needle, wiped the tears away with her apron, and began to sew as she told a story.

"Long time ago, when I live in Miss'ssippi, I work for ol' man Rogers raisin' his chil'ren. By the time I marry Edgar and move to Livin'ston, Doc Rogers' son, Doc Junior, growed up and have family of his own. He want me to come work for him. My oldes' daughter, Sarah, was 'bout seven. Those firs' years, I come home right often to see my chil'ren, and it wont too much of a hardship on me or the chil'ren."

"But then me and Edgar's boy Guicy, then three more after Sarah and a pair of twins, Lord help me." She looked at me and said, "The girl twin, that be your mama, gal." I felt a little thrill to be linked to the story. "That was seven chil'ren. Edgar couldn' hit a lick at a snake 'cause of his arthritis and consumption and all. Sarah, bein' the eldes', have to take care of the young 'uns. It was a right shame, but it was the only way. I have to go work; how else I gone feed them all?"

"'Twas already hard on us, and then the Rogers fam'ly growin', so they keep needin' me more 'n more. I get home less and less, and ev'rythin' keep gettin' wurs. Lord that be a hardship. Let me tell you, it was a long, hard road 'twixt that Rogers place in Laurel, Miss'ssippi and my home in Livin'ston. I grow mighty weary and my heart ache for my po' chil'ren. But I have to earn money, and I tellin' myself that all my hard work goin' to give them a better life."

Grandma regretted the circumstances of how Sarah's childhood was taken away from her. By the time she was a teenager, she'd taken care of her siblings and her father. Sarah resented her fate, and her mother for leaving her to it. She couldn't understand. All she knew was that she'd been sacrificed. Grandma had no idea her daughter was suffering.

"Why, it got so bad, time I come home, Sarah wont say nary word to nobody. She jus' slump 'round the place, glowerin' and sulkin'. Me and Edgar jus' think that a young-un bein' a young-un, and we didn' pay her no mind. I jus' tryin' to cheer ev'rybody up with funny stories 'bout my babies back in Miss'ssippi. Lord, that jus' throwin' oil onto the fire."

When Grandma returned to work one night, Mrs. Rogers went into labor. She said everything went wrong from the start. "Her water break early and wurs' all, that po' li'l chile was tryin' to come into the world the wrong way. She was in mighty bad shape. I think that baby wont gone make it. Doc Rogers say the baby wont gone turn all twisted up in there. Missus Rogers lettin' out some mighty powerful screamin'." Grandma said she was there doing everything she could. "Doc Rogers there tryin' to turn this po' chile, but that baby wont budge at all."

"Doc Rogers work on d'liverin' that baby for a long time. Missus Rogers hold on to that bedpost for dear life. I sit there in the night rubbin' her forehead while Doc workin' on her mighty fierce. Then jus' like outta nowheres, Missus Rogers let out a scream so loud it prac'ly split my ears. That li'l baby girl slip in this world like she know where she goin'. A big baby girl lookin' jus' like her mama. Li'l Victoria."

"Me and Doc Rogers jus' sit there lookin' at that baby, then take her and lay her on her mama's belly. Missus Rogers look plum tuckered out. She barely lif' her eyes to look at that li'l baby girl. Her skin pale as it can be, white as a sheet. Then jus' like light'nin', Missus Rogers start slidin' from this world. She look like she get the conniptions, sha-kin' and a moanin'. Doc Rogers give her some revivin' medicine, but nothin' work. Lord knows Doc done ev'rythin' to save her. She leave this here world that night."

Grandma said she somehow felt responsible for her death, even though there was nothing she could've done. She was stricken. Doc Rogers fell into a deep mourning. Grandma couldn't seem to rebound from the loss. Her pity for poor little Victoria mixed in with her grief. She felt that if she lavished extra love and attention on the baby, it'd make up for everyone's loss. Grandma stayed longer in Laurel with Victoria than she ever had before, and the time slipped by.

It couldn't have come at a worse time. When she returned to Livingston, Sarah was gone. She'd run off with a boy named Cephus. Grandma Lula was devastated. All her sacrifice had been in vain; all her trudging back and forth and spending long, soul-numbing days in some-one else's house had come to naught. She was grievously wounded. She had lost her daughter, who she now realized must hate her. "She throw 'way all my sacrifices. That gal break my heart somethin' fierce."

As Grandma stared at the red and white plaid cloth, she said Mrs. Rogers had bought that material right after she got pregnant with Victoria. She wanted to make matching dresses for the new baby and her two older girls, if the new baby was a girl. "Them dresses wont nev'r made."

Rain began to fall. Grandma appeared to be somewhere far away from that front yard. Aunt Bessie and I were silent. Grandma held the last red and white swatch of cloth in one hand and a needle and thread in the other. I wanted her to sew this piece of fabric into the body of the quilt to create a sense of closure, help heal her wound. But she put that piece of fabric back into the bag, and put the quilting things away.

CHAPTER 11

MOSES THE INSTIGATOR

Grandpa Edgar often sat nearby whittling while Grandma and I were in the yard quilting. He'd cut little branches with his pocketknife and turn them into toothpicks. Sitting there in the sun, sucking on those twigs, he was happy just to be near Grandma. The two of them had been together a long time and had been through so much.

One cloudy day when Grandpa was laid up indoors with his ailments, Grandma rooted around in her sack and pulled out three pieces of cloth for my quilt. One was black-and-white striped. The other was black-and-white with small double X's, and another was black-and-white with a burst of gray. After carefully measuring each piece, Grandma gently wiped the cloths with her hand, ironing out their wrinkles. Her eyes closed like she'd gone into a deep trance. She murmured the name Moses Faulkner. "This here is Moses's shirt." We sat silent under that old oak tree for a while before Grandma began telling the story of Moses.

"Moses was my firs' husband. We only court for a time b'fore we jump the broom. I was sev'nteen and still grievin' Ella and Mama and Papa when I meet Moses. He tall as ev'r can be and he have manners to boot. Them green eyes jus' 'lectric and he talk you 'round in circles and get you to give him your las' nickel, and then your draws and shoes too. He smart as a whip; don' know where he get all that learnin' but he know ev'rythin', like he be a teacher or somethin'. Hooo, boy, I was like the moon and stars and he like the sunshine to me. Lord I jus' love that man. He was fifteen years older'n me, but I didn' have no fam'ly to objec' to his age or warn me 'bout his doin's."

"Moses' mama was a White woman, the daughter of Ol' Man Faulkner, who get pregnant with one of the Colored hand. She desp'rate to keep that baby secret; she try to make one of the maids say the baby come from one of the Coloreds that live in one of the shanties 'cross the way. Her papa find out what she be up too and all hell break loose. He done drag her outta that house, dirt flyin', hollerin' and screamin' all ov'r the place, and tell her to get. Them nightriders track down Moses' Papa. She end up leavin' that baby right there in the kitchen in the big house. One of the maids bring him on down to the shanty and that's where he raise. So he didn' have no real fam'ly."

Grandma said they had a fast courtship. They married and set up house in a small, two-bedroom cottage nestled among the oaks and honeysuckle. As she sewed Moses' shirt into the quilt, Grandma took on a glow. "Moses love my quilts. We spread one out under the big oak tree and lay on it, and he talk like a poetry man 'bout his dream and what he wanna do with his life. He want to live where ev'rybody treated right and there wont be no op'ression. I still a youngun; I like watchin' the light in his eyes when he talk. I think it jus' wishful talk." Grandma sighed.

"Moses was an instigator. It was 'round 1900 and times were chan-gin'. He say, 'Lula, we tired of White folk hangin' us and killin' our chillun; no more, Lula, no more.' Back then them for'ners were goin' 'round talkin' to Colored folk. They get some Coloreds all riled up and they talkin' 'bout how they goin' to protec' theyself. Yes, Lord, it was a heap of mess goin' on back in them days."

I listened in growing fear as Grandma told me how more and more Blacks became victims of lynchings and beatings. There was Moses, going door to door in the Black bottoms of Alabama, telling folks to arm themselves. He visited many homes under the cover of darkness. While most Black people would never conceive of taking up arms, there were some who did.

"He get so tied up he hardly have time for me. I give him all the line he need, that's how I always been. He jus' come home when he can and we have our precious time together. We climb up in the hayloft and look out on the fields. I still remember it to this day, uh huh. But I livin' scared ev'ryday; though I love his fire for betterment, I know one day I'm gone lose him fo'ev'r."

"Then it all get outta hand. The riots come, lots of bloodshed. That's jus' past 1902. 'Twas terrible. People fightin' and killin' each other right here in our own town. Moses in the middle of all that. I get so scared for him, beggin' him to quit. The White folk wont gone put up with that kind of bizness, but he wont stop." Grandma said she had a dream where Moses was on a white horse. "It like to wrung my heart out. I know it was him ridin' on the glory wagon." A sad, distant look shadowed her face.

I was scared to hear the rest of the story. There were never any happy endings; this one was sure to end up in irreparable heartbreak. As I braced myself, the four o'clock flowers were closing their petals for the day. The stars began to glitter the sky. Grandma looked around and silently began putting away the quilting things. I realized she wasn't going to finish the story. I'd have to go to sleep with that image of Moses in my head, knowing tomorrow I'd find out that he'd met some horrible fate. I was dreading and anticipating the next afternoon session of quilting.

Morning finally came and Grandma went through her regular ritual of pulling out the cloths from the cotton sack, looking for the next piece. As I anxiously waited to hear the end of Moses' story, we added two black and white strips of Moses' shirts to the quilt. It was like even his cloth was protecting those around him. As quickly as the story appeared on Grandma's lips the day before, it disappeared just as fast that morning. It was like Moses never existed. Grandma pulled out a different piece of cloth. She didn't speak about Moses. No mention of Moses Faulkner's life and his death. She just moved on to another story. I was left hanging there like a forgotten sheet on a clothesline, flapping in the wind.

My longing to hear the rest of the story wasn't satisfied until I entered the sixth grade. Our history lessons that Miss Clay taught were always prolific because she told the real stories of Black heroes. Since prominent Blacks were absent from our books, Miss Clay made sure she told stories of people like Frederick Douglas and Harriet Tubman. She'd stand before class and tell stories about local Black heroes who Miss Clay had known or heard about from her family. I was 'all ears' as she weaved those stories into an indelible part of my memory.

Miss Clay was known to be a radical. I remember one time she spent an hour talking about the Livingston, Alabama riots between the Whites and Blacks that began around 1902. The Negros, as Mrs. Clay called Blacks, got fed up with the lynching and beatings. The son of a Negro man was beaten to death by a drunk, White man for being in the wrong place at the wrong time. He was devastated by the loss of his son, but was powerless to do anything. Word spread like wildfire throughout the Black settlement.

According to Miss Clay, there were many Negros too scared, and refused to get involved in this man's tirade. Then, this lone Negro man, who Miss Clay left nameless, was livid due to the torture of this man's son.   He vowed to take up arms against the person responsible for the death of this teenage boy. That nameless man became a local hero, a pillar in the Negro settlement. He'd fan out over the countryside preaching about the atrocities committed against Negros. Often times, his rants fell on deaf ears.

When Miss Clay spoke about him, her passion was contagious and spread throughout the room. She said that although there was obvious apprehension in the Black settlement, there were many folks who tired of their family and neighbors being maimed and killed due to the color of their skin. When he assembled enough Negro men together, they'd meet at Zion Hill and Christian Valley churches to talk about their plight. The preachers of those churches didn't like hearing about violence under any circumstances and vowed not to take part in violence of any kind. As a result, that Negro and his men had to meet at secluded locations in the woods to strategize.

In 1903, there was another uprising unlike anyone had ever seen. Negros and Whites were burning and fighting each other like a full-on war had been declared. Many homes and churches were burnt to the ground. Negros had posses' and vigilantes and so did the Whites. Some affluent Whites were financing Negros who had to escape up north because of their involvement in these so-called Black militias. That went on for months, and just as quick as the commotion began, it ended just as abruptly. The nameless Negro man disappeared off the face of earth.

I guess Miss Clay wanted us to understand the moral of the story: you have to fight for what you believe in regardless of the circumstances. She always presented stories and lessons that weren't in history books and defied stereotypes that were continuously heaped onto Black folks. She wanted to make sure we were aware of the many Blacks who made important contributions to this country.

While listening to Miss Clay's story of the 1902 and 1903 uprisings, my mind immediately flashed back to the story of Moses Faulkner. I couldn't help but think he played some kind of role in this upheaval. For all I knew, the man without a name could've been Moses Faulkner, leader among men. He fit the mold of a person who wouldn't hesitate to fight for the cause of the liberation of Black people. In the back of my mind, I was still searching for closure in the Moses Faulkner story. I stood at the crossroads of wondering whether to tell Grandma this story or just let her memories remain as they were.

CHAPTER 12

GRANDPA EDGAR

Grandma spent the rest of the morning talking about Grandpa Edgar. Not to minimize Grandpa's life story, but in no way could it rival that of Moses Faulkner.

"Your grandpa a real ladies' man. He tall and straight, and have a fine purty face. Why, all fifteen of his sistahs and brutha's was some fine lookin' men and women, and believe you me, they all walk 'round like they know it, too. Your grandpa have one older brutha but he die young. After that, your grandpa like the pa for all the younger chil'ren."

"When I meet Edgar, he was jus' comin' from N'orleans. Years b'fore I meet him, he been hoboin' 'round on them box car trains. That's how he end up in N'orleans workin' in the sawmill. He meet his firs' wife Callie there." Grandma said that was some kind of sad situation he had back then. "She die when they wont marry for a good year. Edgar say she catch the plague."

"Back then they didn' know what to do with Colored folk when they gets the plague. They can't go to the White hospital, so they jus' go see the root doctor down in the swamps. Most time all the Colored folk with the plague be all pile up together in one or two li'l shanties. They pack in there like slaves on a slave ship. They lay there and try to keep livin' off roots and herbs. Ain't no White doctor comin' down

88

in them swamps lookin' after no Colored folk with the plague. After they die they jus' burn they bodies up." I found out later that the plague Grandma was referring to was Tuberculosis.

"Your grandpa so young when he marry Callie. After she die, he gets a job in the sawmill. You see, that why Edgar don' have no big toe. He say the train run ov'r it, but I knows he got it cut off in the sawmill. He grieve so 'bout Callie. He jus' wont right in the head, so he spent years jus' hoboin' 'round. Well, one day he get to hoboin' and come into Miss'ssippi. Thats when I meet your grandpa. The firs' time he lay eyes on me he say, "Woman, you one tall drank of water and I like to take a sip." I thought this man done los' his mind."

"After a spell, we start courtin'. He tells me the truth 'bout his wife dyin' and he been hoboin' here and there for the past ten years. He say he and Callie didn' have a chance for chil'ren but he have three other chil'ren' 'twixt Miss'ssippi and Alabama. All that foolin' 'round but didn' marry none of they mama's." Grandma said she practically raised Grandpa's three outside children. She treated them so much like her own that I didn't realize, until she told me, that some of my aunts and uncles I'd come to know and adore, were not her biological children. "Your Uncle Guicy? I raise him from a li'l boy. He wont my blood chile, but close 'nough." That was the way of the world for a lot of country folks. You didn't always know who and how the family relationship scale played out.

"Now that ol' Josh Horn beg Edgar not to marry me 'cause of me bein' dark-skin and all. Hmph. Josh so angry when Edgar marry me anyways, he wont let us nowheres near his ol' house." When I arrived in the country, my dark complexion stood out, too. I remember folks would come by the house and say to Grandma, "That gal looks jus' like you, Miss Lula, dark skin and all."

Grandma Lula instilled me with the virtue of possessing beautiful dark skin. For anyone who came along and equated dark skin with something negative, Grandma was right there to counteract those comments with a positive comeback. She'd say, "The blacker the berry, the sweeter the juice" or "good black don' crack". A lot of people's self-esteem was destroyed after being ridiculed because of their dark skin. Grandma had a way of making sure I loved what God gave me.

"That Josh, color struck as he can be, but Mama Alice wont nothin' like ol' Josh. She give me all these here dress pieces I'm gone put in your quilt. See how nice it fit right here next to Callie's pink handkerchief that your grandpa carry 'round in his pocket as a snot rag all them years? I done wash it and now we gone put it right here." When Grandma finished the story of Grandpa and Callie, I learned something new and interesting about Grandpa. This soothed my spirit for a little while, but I was still craving to know the unfinished story of Moses Faulkner.

It was a nice ending to the day. Evening arrived and we took down the quilting horse. Grandpa made his way out to the front yard. "Edgar, you waitin' on me to fix your nine o'clocker, ain't you ol' man?" This was usually the time when they both launched into their comedy routine, which I think was for my benefit.

Grandpa would say, "Firs', Im a g'wine go see a man 'bout a horse, but I be back direc'ly." This was Grandpa's way of saying he was going to the "john." And Grandma would say, "I'm gone fetch you some of that tu'pentine 'n' sulpha 'lixir 'cause I know your chest gone be tight as Dick's headband by the time you finish seein' john and that man 'bout that horse." Grandpa would mumble something under his breath.

"Talk up Edgar, can't make outta word you sayin'." "I den tol' ya I'm g'wine to see a man 'bout a horse ol' woman! You's gettin' def is me." Grandma would say "Edgar, you been tryin' to get to the outhouse for a spell now, and you ain't made it yet?" I'd fall off my chair laughing so hard my belly hurt. Grandpa would take the last word with, "Woman, you crazy as a fox!" He'd start off towards the outhouse, leaving us laughing like a couple of loons.

"Now, me and Edgar been together a long time and nary a cross word nev'r pass twixt us. All them years I nev'r call him a fool or a lie. I thank the Lord for him ev'ry day." I could see what Grandma meant; I couldn't imagine them ever being apart. They doted on each other and worked together like two pieces of a whole.

CHAPTER 13

MISS DAISY

Apink house with a rusted orange tin roof sat in the backyard of Bethel Hill Elementary School, right next to the playground. The boards were rotted, the paint was peeling, and it was an eyesore. That was Miss Daisy's place, a Juke Joint for folks who were looking for a good time. That was regular gossip for Grandma's visitors who always complained about "all that sinnin' goin' on" right next to the school-house. Of course, this was fodder for Aunt Bessie's lips.

When we went outside for recess, the smell of old liquor hung in the air like wet clothes from the night before. We'd see drunks stumbling out of Miss Daisy's in the morning just as we arrived at school. Miss Daisy was young, but I guess living that sort of life had aged her pretty well. Her face showed signs of deep trouble and her long red hair was streaked with gray. You could tell at one time she'd been a beauty. I might've been young, but my senses told me Miss Daisy wasn't quite right.

She provided a lot of entertainment during our recesses watching the goings-on over there. Grandpa's cousin Bennie was one of Miss Daisy's regular patrons. He didn't drink a little. He drank until he couldn't stand up. We'd see Miss Daisy holding up Cousin Bennie so he wouldn't fall flat on his face. Most times, they'd both fall down right in the middle of the road just from the weight of him. We watched in amazement as they'd fumble their way up from the ground, both their faces covered in rich, white Alabama sand. We laughed so hard our sides split.

Sometimes while the other kids were playing games, I'd hide behind the mulberry tree and watch Miss Daisy. She'd be sitting on the stoop in front of the old pink shanty, sucking on a Pall Mall cigarette. I knew they were Pall Malls because me and my classmates would sneak over into her yard and pick up the butts; empty red Pall Mall boxes scattered all over the place. We'd walk around with lipstick-stained butts hanging off our lips, pretending we were smoking.

Poor Miss Daisy. She'd sit at the opening of her front door looking forlorn, strands of sandy red hair hanging over one of her eyes like it was hiding her own shame and guilt. I think she panged with a longing to be engaging in our silly games. She never shooed us away, or said a word. She just sat there with the saddest look you'd ever see.

My classmates said mean things about her and cackled wildly with laughter. I felt sorry for her, but I still cracked up when they called her a slut even though I had no idea what it meant. One day, I figured I ought to know since I was laughing my ass off about it, so I asked my friend what a slut was. He couldn't give me a definition, confessing he'd heard his father call her that.

During recess one day, I talked Rhoda into coming with me to peek in the window of Miss Daisy's house. We tried to sneak away, but didn't get away fast enough before we ended up with a trail of other kids following along. We had to turn back. That's when we saw Miss Clay standing on the front steps watching us. From that day forward, I gave up the whole idea of spying. I had to put my curiosity to rest or I might get myself into some big trouble.

Then came the biggest surprise of my young life. Miss Daisy appeared in our front yard clutching an old quilt. You could've knocked me over with a feather. It was even more surprising when Grandma embraced Miss Daisy with the warmth and affection of that big choco-laty hug I thought was exclusively for me. For reasons unbeknownst to me, I felt a tinge of jealousy, a feeling I never had before.

Miss Daisy looked disheveled. Her stringy red hair was jutting out all over her head and tears streaked her face with dirt. Grandma mo-tioned Miss Daisy to sit on the ground between her legs. She reached in her apron pocket and pulled out that raggedy black comb and a clean white handkerchief she gave to Miss Daisy to wipe her face. Grandma began combing Miss Daisy's hair while humming that song that always soothed my spirit. I could tell it soothed Miss Daisy's too. Grandma ran the comb gently back and forth through her tangled strands and lulled Miss Daisy into a deep exhalation of calm.

Grandma was probably the only person in Livingston who'd enter-tain Miss Daisy in their home, let alone, treat her with such tenderness. It was just her way. I watched Miss Daisy hand Grandma her quilt, which looked like it'd been badly burnt. I couldn't figure out a way to get close enough to hear their conversation. Miss Daisy's visit was such a surprise, I forgot all about escaping to my secret place so I could eavesdrop on them. Instead, I sat plastered on the front step trying to act like I was disinterested, even though I was dying to find out what they were talking about.

Grandma spent well over two hours talking with Miss Daisy. She was a soothsayer and never liked to see anyone in pain. When Miss Daisy left, Grandma turned to me and said, "We gone make this here quilt right. We gone take our cloths from that bag and makes Miss Daisy's quilt live again."

I was getting a little big for my britches, and since everyone used the term all the time, and no one ever told me the definition, I blurted out, "Grandma, what did that slut want?" I learned right away that was a word that should never come out of a little girl's mouth. That was the first time I'd seen Grandma's ire; she gave me the double whammy:

a scolding and a spanking. When Grandma used the switch, that meant I screwed up and done some serious shit.

She poured out a scolding that stayed in my head for years to come. She picked a branch from a tree, the kind that bent, but didn't break. It made a swish-swish noise as I was getting it and you wouldn't believe just how bad I was getting it. Bad-mouthing people was a serious offense in Grandma's eyes, something that would never be tolerated, even in jest. That lesson would imprint in my brain for the rest of my life.

A few days later while we were out doing the wash, Grandma told me Miss Daisy's story. Washday in our backyard was like a small version of the laundresses' setup with a pot of hot water, a tub of cool water, a scrub board and a line to dry the clothes. "Now you listen, chile. I'm gone tell you 'bout Miss Daisy. That po' gal had a mighty hard life. She was Rachel Demp's chile. Miss Rachel what they call a spinster 'round these parts; both her mama and papa was from somewheres up north and she have good schoolin' and talk like fancy White folk 'cause she travel lots of places. She was a purty woman with dark skin and nice long black hair."

"She didn' live in the Colored part of town. She live right ov'r near where fancy White folk live. She the only Colored who live there. She a maid for one of the big impo'tant fam'lies in Livin'ston. Ev'rybody say she have fineries and lace and all kinda fancy stuff in her house, but Colored folk in town nev'r set foot inside there. Truth be tol', Miss Rachel, she jus' didn' fit in nowheres. Folk say she as nice as pie and wont uppity at all, but Black folk jus' stay 'way from her, and 'course White folk didn' even think of it.

"But Miss Rachel had a friend, a man friend, who was a White man in town. Most folk say it was the newspaper man. She and her man friend carry on for years 'til one day up pop li'l Daisy. Daisy the spittin' image of the newspaper man. She have fire red hair, pale skin, and a dime-size black mole ov'r one eye. Her papa, the White man, have the same red hair, pale skin, and a black mole in the 'xact same spot where Daisy's was. Well, Rachel see right 'way that there wont no way to hide the truth. She got up early one mornin' and wrap that baby up and put it down on the porch of the firs' house she come to in the Colored part of town. Then she jus' waltz off down the road to Lord knows where."

"'Twas a cold Febr'ary mornin' and that po' li'l chile nearly freeze to death. This ol' woman find that baby, set her by the fire for the longes' time. When she see that chile's red hair and black mole, she know the whole story then and there, jus' like it was writ down. That po' chile was mark by the sin of her mama and papa, and there wont no way she could hide."

Grandma told me about Daisy's childhood. She was raised by a community of people and mistreated by both Blacks and Whites. Black children teased her for being White; Whites teased her for being the child of a whore. She was ridiculed beyond belief; called a bastard so many times she thought that was her last name. Some of the women tried to protect her, but their efforts were doomed from the start.

"Where she end up, is where she lays her head. Time she twelve, she stayin' with a young fam'ly in the Colored settlement. That husband, he did some bad things to her. Not all men folks is nice chile. You got to watch yo'self when you get to be a young woman." She looked at me long and hard.

"His wife nev'r know. Daisy couldn' take it and lit off. But she didn' have nowheres to go and nowheres to live. She jus' scrabble 'round, scrapin' and scroungin' and sleepin' in the woods. She got purty desp'rate, near starve, so she lower herself to get some food to eat." Grandma glanced at me again. I was looking steadily at the ground. "Ol' man Chesterton must a been three time her age, got holt of Daisy and put her in that pink house. He got her drunk all the time so she couldn' do nothin', and he beat her to no end. He bring them customers in. Nobody pay no mind. Maybe she kinda get used to it; I reckon that ol' juke joint was the closes' thing to a home she ev'r have."

"She got worn down and used up. The saddes' thing is that she lose a couple babies on the way, and one chile was born dead. Folk say she was killin' them babies, but that wont true a'tall. She want a chile of her own, somethin' to love, in the wurs' way. Po' Daisy, seem like she couldn' have nothin'." Grandma sighed.

It *was* a sad story. She said now I knew the facts behind the appearances: that Daisy hadn't chosen to be a prostitute; it had been forced on her by circumstances and the situation pained her. She told me I should reflect on that and not judge things by how they seemed to be, especially people. I felt bad for all the mean things I'd said, thought and did about, and to, Miss Daisy.

We got to work on Daisy's quilt right away. The first thing we did was wash it with one of Grandma's special solutions to get rid of the burn smell. Grandma took some material from her bag of rags to replace the sections that were tattered or burnt. She put in enough of the old cloth to make a large double ring pattern spread throughout the whole thing. She said it needed balance; that those old spirits would watch over Daisy and help her get through the trials she was facing and had endured her whole life.

Miss Daisy started coming by to visit Grandma almost every week. She'd sit there talking to Grandma, or listen to her hum as she sewed. It must have been therapeutic for her. I'd watch her as she watched Grandma. I knew that feeling well, how just being around Grandma seemed to heal all the things that hurt.

When we finished, the quilt looked almost brand new. Grandma skillfully weaved vibrant blue, orange, and yellow cloths throughout the whole thing. It was a sight for sore eyes. Grandma wanted to do something special for Daisy since no one ever did. I thought about how that quilt she fixed up for Daisy was probably the nicest thing anyone ever did for her. It was just like Grandma to be kind to those who spent most of their life being misunderstood.

Miss Daisy came by the farm and Grandma handed her the quilt. When she unfolded it, her eyes got as wide and wet as a cornfield on a rainy day. Grandma took Miss Daisy in her ever-loving arms and rocked her like a baby while Miss Daisy whispered, "Thank you, Miss Lula," over and over again. She held that quilt like it was the newborn child she never got to have. When she left, she said she didn't know how she'd ever have survived without Grandma. I knew exactly what she meant.

I watched her walk away and was struck by just how wrong I'd been about her; she wasn't pathetic at all. She was someone who had been through many hardships, a survivor. I looked over at Grandma who was humming and putting away the sewing things. As usual, Grandma had the last word.

CHAPTER 14

My Bloodline

Picking cotton in the sweltering Alabama sun was backbreaking work. I had to pick bags for the inner lining of each quilt. It took about two and a half bags for one quilt, gathered in that God-awful heat. It took five bags for an extra-thick quilt. I shuddered, thinking about the poor folks who spent their lives in the cotton field, making only a few cents on each pound they picked. Fortunately for Grandma, Uncle Guicy and his brothers helped her with the heaviest part of the work.

The cotton sack was as tall as me. I'd have to drag that big sack down row after row. Once I filled my five or six bags, I'd empty them one by one and go through them, literally with a fine toothcomb, to pull out the boll weevils and other insects. This was absolutely the worst, because I hated bugs. I'd also have to pull out all plant material because Grandma said she didn't want the customers getting stuck by cotton shucks. I'd sing while I plucked, and sometimes I'd hear Grandma's voice join mine, even from far away.

We sounded like an orchestra. Her favorite song was the "Sparrow Song," and I'd beg her to sing it. She'd blast off into the song before I could get the words out of my mouth.

I sing because I am happy
I sing because I am free
His eyes are on the sparrow
And I know he watches me.

When I listened, chills ran up and down my whole body. Grandma said those chills were kind spirits passing through. She said that passing through those invisible cobwebs were a sign that I'd walked in the midst of ghosts. Grandma had all sorts of superstitions.

She belted out songs so loud and strong, even the hummingbirds stopped what they were doing and took notice. I couldn't help but sing along. I had learned all the words to the songs in Grandma's invisible songbook; most of them were old Negro spirituals. I knew that singing filled her heart with joy. It did the same thing to me.

One morning when Grandma spread my quilt out in order to pick up where we left off, I couldn't help but notice the new cloth that had been added. I didn't know when this happened because I knew each piece backwards and forwards. That was upsetting to me; it felt like strangers had come into my world.

That was *my* quilt and I felt violated. I tried to ask Grandma in my calmest voice about that new cloth, while I choked back tears. She turned and looked at me with surprise, "You done got you some knowin', gal!" She said she'd sewed these cloths on while I was away, and didn't think I'd notice or mind.

After that, Grandma's stories became more profound and took on a more adult tone as she described people, places and things. Grandma proudly crowned me that day as "havin' wisdom." She discussed the design of quilts and how they were woven together based on relationships. She also explained how the interconnections worked and how the pieces were laid out so they related to all the pieces around them, historically and color-wise. Each piece had to fit into the quilt as a whole. Grandma's quilts were an intricate weave of connections and I became more entwined with every stitch.

The time had come when I asked Grandma to tell me more about my quilt. I knew originally it belonged to my great aunt Ella, but I always sensed a deeper mystery behind it. "Hmm," she said as her hands pulled a piece of cloth closer to her. She began sewing as she gathered her thoughts. I sat up straight in that corncob chair, hungry to hear the next thing that would come out of her mouth. She ruminated for a while, then started talking about Chief Tuskaloosa, who was "one tough Injun" from long ago.

The great Indian Chief came to what we know as Alabama around 1542. He founded the Choctaw and Creek Indian Nations. The Choctaw Indians owned Black slaves and sold them at low prices. These were the slaves who hadn't been bought up at the auctions. It wasn't unusual to enter the Choctaw Nation and see entire families of Africans.

"'Twas long, long ago, a Choctaw squaw bed up with "The Big Afr'can," one of the slaves on the res'vation, and have a chile with him. After she get big with chile, they get sold. All three of them sold to 'Masta Slaughter,' in Alabama. After 'while, he sold them to a man name Mr. Young, in Miss'sippi." He was that brutal slave-owner who I had heard about before.

The Choctaw woman was Grandma Lula's grandmother, Emma's mama. She had four sons and the one daughter, Emma. When I heard this, my eyes went wide. This made Emma half Choctaw and half African. I was part Choctaw! I loved knowing I was connected to the countryside that had become my home.

I was wiggling around when Grandma said, "Are you listenin' to me, gal? If you ain't listenin', I ain't gonna recollec' no more, you hear me?" "Yes'm, Grandma," I said with my head bent low. She went on. "Emma's mama the one who teach Emma to quilt. She already learnt from her Injun people, now she learnt from her papa's folk who learnt they ways from Afr'ca. Emma have all this learnin' runnin' 'round her head – that why her quilts so special."

I wondered if the superstitious side of Grandma's quilt making came from Great Grandma Emma's Indian heritage, a culture that held strong beliefs in the spirit world. They also believed that placing cloths of the dead into the quilt acted as a talisman. These beliefs were passed on to Grandma Lula who integrated her Indian and African culture.

Grandma stopped mid-sentence and asked, "Now what I jus' say to you, chile?" Luckily, the rest of the story was familiar to me: how Emma grew up to marry Joe Young, and I was able to provide the answer. "Um huh," said Grandma, and finished up by saying that of course I knew the end; Emma had two daughters after slavery, Ella and herself, and now I knew where all of us women came from.

She reminded me about the Indian and slave cemetery in the woods on the outer edge of our farm. On a clear day, when the corn crop was done for the year, you could see the fence line that separated the cornfield from the cemetery. Grandpa took me there once. He called it "the ol' time religion cemetery." A few wooden crosses with no names marked the graves. On the other side, there were some Indian artifacts scattered around. He told me I should never set foot on those grounds because they were sacred. And in case that didn't scare the crap out of me, Grandpa also said it was haunted with spirits patrolling the perimeters. Needless to say, that was enough for me to steer clear of that place.

Grandma went on to say that the Indians had lived there since the beginning of time and even though they were driven out by the White folks, people here came from them, their spirits remained, and we should honor them. I felt different after hearing the source of my maternal bloodline. I was part of a lineage that went on from generation to generation, something bigger than myself. I'd never felt that way before.

CHAPTER 15

AUNT TUDNEY

Aunt Tudney was my favorite aunt. She was Grandpa's younger sister. Her given name was Annie Grace Horn Downson and lived just south of my grandparents' farm with her younger sister, my great aunt Money. Aunt Tudney was famous for her "field hollers," the songs that were sung in the cotton fields during slavery times. She'd sing these "ahs" and "ohs," deep and sonorous, syllables that came from the depth of her soul. They were mysteriously haunting and moving, arising from a cavern of pain and suffering. They made me shiver.

I was allowed to go to her house on my own; I'd run the entire mile and a half, taking off barefoot to fly through the cornfields over the bushes, outrunning the deer. I loved feeling the wind on my face and the blood pumping in my veins. At the edge of her property was a huge fence. It was a fight to open, but when I did, I'd jump on the gate and let it swing me with it as it moved. I was always careful to latch it back shut so Aunt Tudney's geese wouldn't get loose.

Inside the gate there was a two hundred foot grassy slope we called the "Horn Grove." I'd tear off down the hill with the wind at my back, throw myself down and roll until I came to a stop. I spit the grass out of my mouth, knocked off the goose shit, and climbed up the other side of the hill to my aunt's house.

Aunt Tudney was one of the few people I was allowed to accept food from. In Grandma's book, taking food from people showed that you had no home training. I was never allowed to accept food from people, relatives included, even if my stomach was rumbling with hunger. Aunt Tudney was an exception to Grandma's rule; I could eat to my heart's desire. She had all kinds of delicious homemade pies and cookies that she kept under her bed. For some reason, a lot of old folks in the south stored pies, cakes and Lord knows what else, under their beds. Maybe to keep them away from hungry, sweet-eating girls like myself.

When I reached the side of the house, Aunt Money was sitting in her wooden swing on the porch. That was her perch. I greeted her, she nodded her head, and that was the extent of our 'conversation.' Aunt Tudney came striding down the dogtrot. I could hear her before I actually saw her. The floorboards squeaked as she came out from the back room. She was a towering woman with a smile that took up her whole face. She had on an apron with big pockets. Her legs and ankles were the size of tree trunks, socks sagging down around her feet. Her backside was so big she had to walk with her hands on her hips and slightly bent over just to balance herself.

Aunt Tudney wasn't obese. She was what folks down south called stout or big-boned. She was married once, but her husband died suddenly and she never married again. I sort of felt sorry for her because she was never able to have children. The house she and Aunt Money lived in was their parents' old house, which had been willed to them when they died.

Entering the big front room was like stepping into a museum. It was always dark because Aunt Tudney kept her windows covered with heavy cloth. There was a gigantic fireplace in the middle of the room. Dried herbs and leaves hung from the rafters and lay in piles all over the place. She used those herbs to make special elixirs for Grandma's rheumatism and Grandpa's asthma. There were colorful quilts stacked up in every corner.

We sat next to the fireplace as I stuffed myself with cakes and cookies and Aunt Tudney told stories, sang and stirred. She was always chewing on a long wooden stem and spitting the juices into the fireplace. Even when she spoke, she sounded like she was singing. She had a powerful voice and loved to belt out songs like Grandma. My favorite one she sang was: "I Wonder Where My Brother's Gone."

I wonder where my brother's gone
Wonder where's my brother John
They say he's gone to the wilderness
And won't come back no more

She'd rock in that rocking chair as it hit the floorboards right on beat. The wooden house echoed with creaks and groans, adding an eerie melody to the song. We must've been a sight, the two of us, rocking side by side in our rockers: one hefty old woman and one tiny young girl just rocking away.

She told me a story about Great Grandpa Josh Horn and his inability to read. He could find a verse in the Bible by memorizing how the words looked, even though he didn't know the difference between an "A" or "C." When he was out and about town talking with the good old boys at Millen's store, he'd look at the verse and repeat it as though he was reading it. She'd howl with laughter recalling the way he'd fool all the White folks who thought Josh could actually read.

She always went on about how White folks loved Papa Josh. She talked about Ruby Tartt and the other Livingston Whites who doted on Papa Josh Horn. It made me uncomfortable. It sounded to me like Josh Horn had been a big "Uncle Tom." I was starting to gain perspective about his situation and realized that growing up as a slave, the only realistic way to survive was by keeping the Whites happy and humored. He sure did obtain a lot of benefits from those Whites: land, money, loans, and special favors. He was no fool.

One day I asked Aunt Tudney about the quilts she had stacked in the big room. A smidgeon of snuff juice trickled down her chin before she caught it with the back of her hand. Those little bird eyes of hers began dancing behind those old droopy eyelids. She got up and shuffled across the room where she pulled a couple of them from the pile.

"You see this quilt here, gal? Well, my mama Alice made this one, and this one, and this one b'fore Papa an' Mama had your grandpa Edgar. She did the quiltin' for Masta Ike Horn and his daughter fo' yeahs." Aunt Tudney pointed out the extravagant lace that lined the outer borders of a fancy quilt. Then she pulled out one with corduroy material in a patchwork of colors and sizes. She handed it to me and said, "This one I gone give to yo', chile." I was speechless, and honored. I sat there for the rest of my visit with that quilt wrapped around me like a second skin, grinning from ear to ear. I couldn't wait to show Grandma my new treasure! When I left, I ran like a bat outta hell to get home. I wore my new quilt like it was a royal cape and I was a queen.

I was so excited that I didn't notice it began to rain. It was one of those days where the sun would peek in and out of dark billowy clouds. I looked up at the sky and saw the biggest rainbow I'd ever seen. I remembered Grandma telling me that at the end of rainbows, there was a pot of gold and I'd have to find the end in order to claim the gold. Whenever I'd see one, I'd take off running, and when I'd come back, Grandma and Grandpa would be side splitting with laughter. Seeing a rainbow out in the country was a splash of magic in an ordinary world. It illuminated the whole sky. I ran faster than a gazelle looking for that pot of gold, using my quilt for wings.

Lost in my fantasy, I didn't notice how dark it was getting as I went flying through the woods. I had no idea how I'd gotten so turned around. To my horror, I realized I was so off track that I'd run right through the middle of the old slave and Indian cemetery, trampling over the artifacts. I didn't know what to do, so I walked home slowly with a feeling of dread hanging over me. All that joy of showing Grandma my new quilt had vanished. When I walked through the front door, she could tell something was wrong, but I was too afraid to fess up.

I moped around indoors for a week, jumping at every little sound. I wouldn't go outside at all. I wouldn't even go into town with Grandpa and Uncle Jeff when they offered to take me. I finally broke down and told Grandma everything, wailing about how I'd be haunted forever by those lost spirits. Grandma nodded seriously as I told her the story.

Then she scared the living daylight out of me by leading me right back into that cemetery. That was the *last* place I wanted to go; I was sure there were angry spirits there ready to drag my ass directly to hell.

Grandma was calm as she kneeled down by the broken-apart graves. She motioned me to kneel beside her. She picked up the pieces I'd tripped over that night and put everything back in their proper place. She began praying to God to restore the integrity of that sacred place. She prayed and prayed and prayed some more, with me sweating it out at her side.

We got up to leave, all stiff and sore from the long vigil, and walked away in silence. When we got some distance away, Grandma said it was okay now, that we made things right. All the same, I never went anywhere near that cemetery again.

CHAPTER 16

THE RETURN FULL CIRCLE

One morning at breakfast, Grandpa started reminiscing about what it was like growing up with fifteen brothers and sisters all living under the same roof. He was laughing about how the boys always tried to get the better of the girls, playing all kinds of tricks, but the girls always outsmarted them. That set me thinking about my own seven brothers and sisters and how I didn't know them at all.

Later that day when we were out in the yard working on my quilt, I told Grandma I was sorry she never knew her brothers or sisters, except for Ella. She grunted, then leaned over and probed around in her bag of rags until she pulled out gold and blue pieces of corduroy. She said, "Well, honey, there jus' lots of things you don' know yet, like 'bout my bruthas Robert and Isaiah." You could've knocked me over with a twig. I'd always thought both brothers had been sold away and disappeared.

I asked her a bunch of questions at once, and she said, "Shush, chile." I immediately shushed. If I didn't, I'd get, "You don' sass grown folk, chile." She settled back into her stitching and told me there was a whole story to the answers of all my questions if I would just be patient.

Grandma was working for Doc Rogers and his wife was still alive. They liked to drive out and pay social calls to other wealthy families around the area. Grandma would accompany them to take care of the children. It was a welcome change for her, as it gave her a chance to sightsee and visit with some of the other Black domestics.

One fine day they were out in the carriage when Grandma overheard them say that the plantation they were going to visit was the Young's plantation. They wanted to pay their respect to Mrs. Young, a distant cousin of Doc Rogers, because her husband, young Mr. Young had passed away. Grandma quaked like the earth itself was shaking. She wanted to throw herself down from the carriage, but managed to pull herself together and stay put.

As they pulled up in front of the Young's house, she never flinched. She showed me how she sat up in that wagon with her head held high. It must've taken all her strength not to run like hell and stay put like nothing was amiss. The huge white front door opened to welcome them, and Grandma's heart was pounding like it would fly right out of her chest and out towards the sky. What would she say to Mrs. Young? Worse yet, would Mrs. Young recognize Grandma? Would she say anything to her? Those were the longest moments of her life, waiting there at that front door.

It was little Patsy who greeted them- little Patsy who worked for the Young's since she was a "li'l gal," and was now grown up. Grandma was relieved. There was no sign of whether or not she recognized Grandma. Patsy took them to a waiting room. They waited for what felt like eternity until finally, the door opened and Mrs. Young, old and grey, came in. Her eyes fell on Grandma. She looked distressed, but turned to greet the Rogers politely. Then she walked over to Grandma and took her hands in hers as she welled up with tears.

The Rogers were taken aback. They had no idea what had transpired so long ago. Grandma was taken aback, too. That was the last thing she expected. Mrs. Young told the story to the Rogers and said she was relieved to be able to unburden herself. She'd been horrified by what her husband did, especially because she was eternally grateful to

Ella for saving her little girl's life when the doctors were unable to help her. Grandma Lula's composure melted a little and a tear leaked out. She was grateful to hear about Ella saving that little girl's life.

Mrs. Young excused herself and took Grandma out back to the little shanty where Grandma lived with her parents and Ella so many years ago. It was a bit run down, but just as it used to be. Mrs. Young held the door open for Grandma. It was hard for her to go inside. When she entered, she was overcome with a thousand feelings. Everything was covered with dust. Mrs. Young walked over to the little table that stood near the cook stove and pulled out a cotton sack. She handed it to Grandma and said, "This belongs to you." Grandma took the bag and saw it was full of cloths. It was the quilting bag that Emma and Ella had used, the same grungy bag Grandma remembered from so long ago.

"I have something else for you," Mrs. Young spoke in a soft voice. She led Grandma to a room off the back porch where Mrs. Young pulled out a large painting of Ella as a young woman. She was wearing a white dress and hat. Grandma's jaw must've dropped to the floor. "Missus Young, Lord where on earth...?" Apparently a friend of the Young's had made that painting years ago. Mrs. Young returned to her guests and they went on with their visit. Grandma carefully wrapped up the painting with trembling hands and put it away in the carriage. She went to find her young charges, who kept her distracted for the rest of the visit.

When it was time to leave, everyone said goodbye. As the carriage was about to pull away, Mrs. Young went up to Grandma and whispered in her ear that she knew the fate of her two brothers. Grandma nearly fell off that carriage. Mrs. Young told Grandma that the boys had been sold to a Mr. Matthews. Both of them had run away, but she thought they were still alive. Mrs. Young said she wasn't sure what happened to Grandma's sisters.

As the carriage jerked forward, Grandma sat there motionless. She couldn't believe it had been kept secret from her for this long. She was bubbling over with joy at the possibility of finding her brothers. It took a while for reality to set in. Grandma knew all too well that the conditions of slavery were harsh. Slaves often died or disappeared, and record keeping was non-existent. Finding her brothers would be like finding a needle in a haystack.

She searched in every way possible. She tried to trace them to the Matthews plantation, but found nothing. Doc Rogers tried assisting her with his wide net of connections, but every search yielded a dead end. She continued searching for years. Even after she finally gave up, she'd occasionally run across something that would instigate another attempt. Her lost brothers were always on her mind.

Grandma took the pieces of fabric we sewed into my quilt from Isaiah and Robert's black and red gingham shirts. I suddenly had a better understanding of this precious bag of cloths. I would never refer to it as a "bag of rags" again. I thought about the importance of Grandma entrusting me with the quilt and all these stories. Not only did I have to remember it, but I also had to hold it sacred.

That story got me thinking about how I was the keeper of the secret of Aunt Tudney's money. Like most old Black folks, Aunt Tudney didn't believe in banks; she buried her money instead. She was always careful not to be seen, but everybody knew she'd dug a hole somewhere on that land and her money was in it. One time when I went to visit her, I came through the gate and happened to look down into the Horn Grove. There was Aunt Tudney, bent over. All you could see was ass for days. Grass and dirt were flying all over the place. She was planting her money so deep in the ground you'd think she'd start watering it to see if it'd grow.

She glanced around suspiciously and I ducked out of sight. It was pure happenstance that I caught her in action. I'm sure no one else ever knew where her stash was; not even Aunt Money. Aunt Tudney had gotten so old that she couldn't remember where she buried that money. Try as they might, none of the aunts and uncles or cousins could find it. I thought about telling them where it was hidden just to see all the trouble that'd ensue when it was found. Instead, I decided it best to honor Aunt Tudney's memory and let her money lie where she left it.

CHAPTER 17

GRANDMA SUGAR BABE

Grandma and I were shelling crowder peas one evening when out of the clear blue, she said it was time for me to get to know my other kinfolk. To be more specific, it was high time I met Grandma Sugar Babe. That threw me for a loop; I often heard Grandma and Grandpa talk about Grandma Sugar Babe and assumed that they were talking about Miss Sugar. She was my father's mother living not too far away. "Pert'near Miss'ssippi," Grandma said before singing a little jingle while laughing:

> *M-i-crooked letter, crooked letter i,*
> *Crooked letter, crooked letter i,*
> *Humpback, humpback i*

The "crooked letters" were "S" and the humpbacks were "P". I was willing to bet no one from Mississippi *ever* pronounced the extra S's or I's in Mississippi. Grandma said she thought that little song came from slavery times; a clever way for slaves to learn how to spell.

"Since you always 'round Edgar's people, be a good thing you learn some of your daddy folk. And you big 'nough now, you can go stay with your grandma Sugar Babe for a spell." When folks in the country used the term "a spell" in relation to time periods, it could mean a few hours or a few years. I'd never been away from my grandparents' house for any period of time. My tears rushed up at the ready and I asked if I'd be coming back.

She bellowed out a laugh at my dramatics and said, "Chile, you comin' back to Grandma; nobody want you but the dev'l!" That made her laugh even louder. She thought it was so funny, pretty soon I was laughing right along with her. "Now, don' you worry, you gone have a big ol' time. And you gone be back b'fore you know it."

She packed me a little bag. Miss Sugar was entrusted with delivering me safely to Grandma Sugar Babe's house. Before we left, Grandma gave Miss Sugar a stern warning about what she was to do and how she was to take care of her Grandchild. Otherwise there'd be hell to pay. You didn't want to cross Grandma, believe you me; even Miss Sugar perked right up when she was being stern.

When we left, my anxiety turned to excitement. This was the first time I'd ever ridden with Miss Sugar. Somehow, I knew that before we'd reach our destination, slick and sly Miss Sugar would have something up her sleeve that would boggle the mind. With Miss Sugar, you just never knew the shenanigans she'd conjure up. Sure enough, as soon as we got around the bend and out of Grandma's sight, Miss Sugar brought the car to a screeching halt. All I saw was white sand flying.

Miss Sugar said, "Come on, li'l nigger, get behind the wheel; let me see what you got." I could've messed my pants right there in the front seat. Those bright eyes flashed at me as Miss Sugar repeated, "C'mon gal, get your li'l ass ov'r here and drive!" Crazy as it was, within ten minutes, she had me driving like a pro. You could barely see my pea-sized head as I sat in that car grinning a mile long while Miss Sugar cackled like an old hen.

I felt like her husband Tank. When she told me to stop, I stopped. When she told me to slow down or speed up, I did just that. It felt so good to be doing the unimaginable. Miss Sugar let me drive until we reached the Moore place past Bethel Hill. That's when she told me to pull over. I could barely reach the pedals and my feet were telling me to keep going. By the time Miss Sugar said it for the third time, she was screaming. "Stop the damn car, nigger!"

Grandma Sugar Babe lived in a dead end town called Pine Grove, Alabama, right next to the Mississippi line. When we got there, we discovered that Pine Grove was appropriately named. Everywhere you looked there were pine trees and pinecones.

We drove up to Grandma Sugar Babe's house and saw her sitting on the front porch shelling peas. When Miss Sugar got out of the car, instead of saying "Good afternoon," she said, "Somebody need to clean up these damn pine cones; shit's everywhere, messin' up the tires on my car!"

Grandma Sugar Babe was so taken aback by Miss Sugar's ballsy behavior that she barely noticed me. I wasn't offended because I knew Miss Sugar had that effect on people.

When she finally realized I was there, she greeted me with a wide smile and a big hug. She was my father's mother, but since I didn't remember what my father looked like, I couldn't tell if there was a resemblance, even though I was looking for one.

Grandma Sugar Babe was a short, dark-skinned woman with gray hair braided in two plaits. She had a black mole over her eye, which made me think of the story of Miss Daisy. She smiled continually as she offered us glasses of ice water. We sat on the front porch in wooden swings, Miss Sugar on one side swinging away, and me and Grandma Sugar Babe on the other side sharing the other swing.

Miss Sugar took her teeth out of her mouth, popped them in the water, and began stirring her teeth round and round with her finger. Grandma Sugar Babe and I watched this until I felt myself dizzy. She talked the whole while about men who had "done did her wrong," and sung phrases of the blues as she continued to twirl her teeth around in the glass. She'd never even met Grandma Sugar Babe before, but she let it all out anyway. It was just her way.

Miss Sugar noticed the looks we had on our faces and said, "What's wrong with ya'll niggers, you act like you ain't nev'r seen nobody with plate teeth!" One thing I knew for sure was that when Miss Sugar took out her teeth, her regal looks and beauty collapsed. I thought to myself how she should never, ever do that again! She popped her teeth back in, wiped the water off her hands on the side of her dress, gave me a hug and told Grandma Sugar Babe to take good care of me. She slipped behind the wheel of her car and sped away with pinecones crunching under her tires.

As usual, Grandma Lula was right. I had fun staying at Grandma Sugar Babe's. I had so much fun that I forgot to be homesick. Grandma Sugar Babe loved sweets and always had plenty of cake, cookies and candy readily available. We'd sit in the swing together and I'd eat until I'd bust a button. I drank cola's, sometimes two a day because Grandma Lula would never let me do that.

Grandma Sugar Babe smiled all the time. Even when she frowned, she was smiling. Boy, did she love to laugh. I'd make funny faces and just like Grandpa, she'd laugh so hard it looked like it hurt. In the mornings when I got up, she'd be up cooking breakfast and smiling about nothing I could figure out. My favorite thing about staying at Grandma Sugar Babes' besides the cola was that I didn't have any chores.

Her old mother, Grandmella, lived in her own little room off the side of Grandma Sugar Babe's house. Grandmella was so old she had a full-grown gray beard. The first time I saw her, I nearly dropped in my tracks at the sight of a woman with a grown man's beard. She was a kind and gentle soul, and very knowledgeable about insects. Even though I hated bugs, I liked how much she knew about them.

One of the best things at Grandma Sugar Babe's house was the fabulous wooden swing on her front porch. Unlike Grandma's front porch, which was screened, Grandma Sugar Babe's was wide open so you could swing as high as heaven. Flying through the air made me feel like a bird. I'd swing for hours until I wore myself out completely, falling asleep right there in that old swing.

Deep inside an afternoon nap one day, I was jarred awake by the hot air of someone's breath in my face. I opened my eyes to see three little white faces, not two inches away from my nose. I thought I was dreaming and reached out to poke at one of the little faces with my finger. It laughed. Then I heard Grandma Sugar Babe calling and the three of them went running inside the house, giggling. When I followed, Grandma Sugar Babe gave us all cheese sandwiches and we stood around eating them not quite sure knowing how to act.

I'd never seen little White kids up close before. When we gobbled down the sandwiches, Grandma Sugar Babe said, "G'wine and git a dipper of water from the well to wash down dat cheese. Ya'll don' wanna get the piles, now do ya? " The four of us took off running towards the well, racing to see who would get there first. I won. I grabbed the bucket and heaved it down the well into the cool water; then I used the attached chain to pull it up, with the water splashing over the edges. I filled the dipper with the ice-cold water and drank, half of it falling on my feet. Boy did that feel good when it trickled through my toes. I handed the dipper to the first little boy and he drank and passed it on until each of us had gulped down our fill. After that, we were friends. We spent the rest of the day playing house and pretending to be princes and princesses, something they had to teach me about.

During the two weeks I was there, I spent every waking hour with those kids. We joshed, ran around, and made mud cakes. There were a lot of pinecone games. I had never had that kind of freedom and companionship before. Grandma Sugar Babe told me that these were "practic'ly my own granchillun." They were Armstrong's from the Armstrong family, a wealthy old family in Pine Grove. Grandma Sugar Babe's husband had worked for them, as did his father, and they rented their land. The Armstrong's never let any crazy White folks mistreat them.

She told me how her husband died of a heart attack before he was forty, leaving her with a large debt to the store in town. The storeowner declared his intention to confiscate all her possessions, including her cow. Sugar Babe turned to Old Man Armstrong, who tried to dissuade the storeowner. When he wouldn't budge, Armstrong went over to Grandma Sugar Babe's farm and moved her cow over to his place so the owner couldn't take it.

When it was time for me to leave, those little White kids acted like their hearts were broken. They came over and found me packing up all the goodies that Grandma Sugar Babe gave me to smuggle home. When I told them I was leaving, they burst into tears. I was speechless. That was the first time I had ever had that effect on anyone. I could see that our time together had been special for them. It had been special for me, too. Before I knew it, I was bawling my eyes out, too.

We dragged my bag outside. I hugged Grandma Sugar Babe good-bye. We all stood together in a little group, crying and hanging on to each other. We must've looked ridiculous carrying on like that. Miss Sugar's car rolled down the driveway and when she got close, the look on her face said it all. She stopped the car and told me to "get your skinny li'l ass in the car" because she had a treat for me. I had to shut my damn mouth if I wanted it. One thing about Miss Sugar: she acted gruff, cussed and said outrageous things, but that was just how she expressed her love.

I gave Grandma Sugar Babe another big hug and climbed into the car. Even though I was sad to leave Grandma Sugar Babe and my new little White friends, I was glad to be going back to Livingston. I couldn't wait to see Grandma Lula. I didn't realize how much I needed her until I wasn't with her. There was no way I was going to let anyone know that because I wanted to be able to go back again next time.

CHAPTER 18

MISS HATTIE

Grandma's hands told the story of her life. There were years of toil in her fingers from working in the fields, washing, cleaning, and quilting. She was eighty-two years old, yet she continued to rise before daybreak every morning to farm and feed the cows. Each of her fingers was rough with calluses and her feet were probably just as bad off. Her insides were probably the same. That old woman had been through holy hell in her life.

I'd see her coming in from the fields around noontime, wiping the sweat from her brow and walking heavy with fatigue. I could hear her singing old Negro spirituals as she crossed the pasture. It was such a beautiful sound, signifying the end of her long, hard workday.

Grandma Lula was old fashioned and held close to her old ways. She wasn't about to change for anyone or anything. She and Grandpa Edgar finally let their home be wired for electricity, but Grandma Lula still chose to light candles and lanterns at night instead of using the new electric lights. She was old school all the way.

Then came a bit of news: we finally acquiesced to modern technology. Uncle Guicy bought my grandparents a television. I was so excited I jumped up and down like someone put fire ants in my drawers. At first, there was no way Grandma was going to let that television be in the front room. She didn't allow people in that room except under special circumstances. In my mind, a television was definitely a special circumstance. Grandma relented. After all, she was a big old softy. We only got one channel. I remember it well; channel 11. It came on at 11:00 am and went off air at 11:00 pm. Grandpa was the only one allowed to touch the television. He was also the designated on/off and turn-the-channel person. Grandma said no one else knew how to operate it.

Grandma and I would bring our quilting in from the yard and into the front room so we could watch the soap operas *Search for Tomorrow* and *Guiding Light*. The television went off after the soaps were over and wouldn't go back on until the six o'clock news was on. After that, it was turned off for the rest of the night. Sundays were different because we'd watch the Ed Sullivan Show, which ended around eight o'clock.

I went to school and loved bragging about my television set, just like all the other kids. I was happier than a pig in shit. The only problem was the television came on the last day of school so I only had one day to brag. I'd have to keep my little boasting self in check until September.

I had just finished the seventh grade and was a full grade ahead of other kids my age. Down in the country there was no middle school. You started high school in eighth grade. Miss Clay had high hopes for me. With straight A's, she knew I'd be going on past high school to do great and wonderful things.

On the last day of class, before I walked out of those schoolhouse doors for the last time, Miss Clay took me aside. In her most schoolmarm voice she told me, "Phyllis, you must walk straight ahead and never turn around to look at the footsteps you walked in yesterday because those footprints won't fit your feet anymore." She gave me a big hug before I walked away ready to do great and wonderful things.

The summer stretched out before me. My quilt was nearly complete. It was only missing a few pieces. It was so beautiful with its multi-colored cloths running in contrasting diagonals. It carried the stories of my ancestors, stories I knew intimately, and was stitched by the loving, hardworking hands of my grandma Lula. It was a treasure beyond all treasures.

We took out the quilt to sew in the last few pieces and spent time admiring it so far. "Right nice," said Grandma. "Guess this'll finish it up." She put her finger out and traced the length along the sides. She was visually measuring how these pieces would link to the first piece and complete the pattern. Then she looked at me, as if reflecting on how far I'd come since we began. She pulled out several pieces of cloth. "These're special pieces," she said with her voice a little tight. She cleared her throat and began to sew. When she was ready, she spoke.

"I knew Miss Hattie back in Laurel, Miss'ssippi. She was older'n me, but we good friends. Hattie was the spittin' image of my sistah Ella. She look like my papa jus' spit Hattie out. Fac' a the mattah, Hattie coulda been my sistah, since nobody ev'r know much 'bout where my mama's chil'ren are after they get sold; they coulda been anywhere, includin' Laurel. The only thing I know 'bout them is what Missus Young tol' me 'bout my bruthas."

"Hattie work for the judge takin' care of his house and his chil'ren. She live right on the edge of town in a purty li'l house with her three young chil'ren. She know how to put the roots on folk. Puttin' the roots on folk was some serious bizness and it was few folk in b'tween who can do it. My mama tol' me 'bout root doctors who come from Afr'ca. Folk purty much steer clear of Miss Hattie, whether they White or Colored."

Grandma said she heard the story that Hattie caught her husband laid up in bed with another woman. Miss Hattie supposedly put urine in his collard greens. He thought it was strong vinegar and downed those greens like it was his last meal. The next thing you know, he just keeled over and died right there at the dinner table. After that, no one wanted to come near her.

"I doted on Hattie's chil'ren. I took 'em when Hattie was busy. I love to do for them. This was way b'fore I have my own chil'ren. They grow right fond of me, too. Me and Hattie get real close. I even get her to join the church choir with me and Leontyne Price's mama; Lord, the look on people's faces! Hattie's boy Seth, now that boy sho' nuff a firecracker! He smart as a whip, and that boy didn' mind lettin' you know either. He think he was the man of the house and he work hard as a full-grown man. I 'spose he have sense, considerin' the situation; he have a houseful of women to reckon with."

"He work fo' ol' man Springer, in the orchard. In the fall time, he shake them pee-con trees and gather and load 'em up into big silver cans. In springtime, he glean the persimmon trees. Now you best be careful when you glean persimmons 'cause if they ain't ripe, they make your mouth pucker up so bad you think you done suck yo'self inside out. So he have to be careful to pick jus' the ripe ones."

"Now, Mr. Springer have a li'l granddaughter; a tiny gal 'bout the size of you when you firs' come here. This li'l gal turn up from time to time. She run ov'r and play with Seth. One time they out in that orchard when Seth get a no good fo' nothin' idea; he gone give her some unripe persimmon. No, ma'am, she wont have none of that. So Seth, bein' a li'l dev'l, take a bite out of it hisself, show her how good it is, and make a face like it better'n candy. 'Course then *she* have to try it. She bite into that mess, and let me tell you, she sound like the world comin' to the end; she got to hollerin' and carryin' on. Seth laugh and laugh, and then that po' li'l gal run off back home. Seth didn' think no more 'bout it; he finish up his gleanin' and go on home."

Grandma gave me a serious look when I started to laugh, and shook her head "no." She proceeded in a dark voice to tell me what happened next. Apparently, the little granddaughter ran home and told old Mr. Springer what happened. She told him how Seth had bitten the persimmon and then she put it in her mouth to taste it. That just about caused the old White man to have a stroke; that a Black boy had his mouth on something and gave it to his little girl to eat. The Whites in Mississippi were treacherous people. They were well known for committing depraved deeds when it came to Blacks. Even the "hushed blood line" didn't matter much.

"Ol' Mr. Springer go 'round tellin' ev'rybody what happen. They gets all stirred up, make speeches, and the menfolk get a posse to come after li'l Seth. Hattie and her chil'ren was sittin' in they house fixin' supper with the usual hijinks. They in good spirits 'cause they jus' got runnin' water and 'lectricity. Now they was livin' real good. 'Twas a clear night with the sound of crickets and tree frogs all 'round them."

"The Campbell fam'ly who live 'cross the way say they hear the sound of horse comin' near Hattie's house. They say all the sudden they hear them angry White men voices. Mo Campbell say they sound all riled up. Hattie know somethin' jus' ain't right. Them White men screamin' out fo' li'l Seth. Now Hattie she prob'ly try to keep that boy from goin' out there to face them White men. That boy didn' have hardly no fear. I can see it sho' as I'm sittin' here, that boy fightin' with Hattie tryin' to protec' his fam'ly. Hattie know not to go outside. They bang on that door, and bang on that do' some more. Then it get quiet as a church mouse. Quick as lightnin' blazin' bottles of kerosene rags come through them windows and break open on the floor. That ol' house catch afire. Hattie and her chil'ren burnt up. They burnt so bad there won't nothin' lef' but bones."

I could hardly bear to sit there when Grandma finished the story. I'd have to somehow find a way to hold it inside my being. I understood why Grandma saved it. All the previous ones she told had helped build me up into a person who could handle such a thing. Grandma said she saw the spirit of Hattie. This was before word of Hattie's demise spread through the neighborhood of the Black settlement. Grandma was at home when she suddenly felt Hattie's spirit "passing through to glory." Grandma knew right away that Hattie died.

She went on to say, "Nobody ev'r move them ashes of Hattie and her chil'ren from that house. We have a service right there at that burnt down house with me and Leontyne Price's mother, and the rest of the church choir. I get two li'l boy shirts and some li'l girls dresses they lef' at my house when I keep 'em from time to time. Yes Lord, I still get they things right in this here bag. Kep' 'em all this long time."

She closed her eyes and began to sing her favorite song- a song for Hattie and her children.

His eyes are on the sparrow
and I know he watches me.

In the center of my quilt were pieces of Seth's gray shirt and Gloria and Elizabeth's blue dresses. They were the pieces that completed the repair of my quilt. As I sat there digesting their story, I wrapped that quilt around me, feeling the pain and injustice of all those who passed on, all who endured more than I could ever imagine. Their memory kept alive in a hand stitched mosaic of love that would live on forever in a piecing together of what I used to call rags.

CHAPTER 19

TAKEN AWAY AGAIN

Summer on the farm meant morning hours in the field with Grandma, plucking snap peas off the vine, walking down endless rows of freshly plowed dirt, and picking Grandma's freshly-turned ice potatoes, commonly known as Irish potatoes. Ninety-plus degrees and dripping with humidity. Sometimes our old mule, Bob, plopped right down in the middle of the row and lie there in the heat; not moving an inch until he was ready to move.

Bob carried on with a habit of lying around on the job for weeks, until Grandma had enough. She was beginning to fall behind on her other chores so she had Uncle Herman bring in his mule, Chastity. When Bob saw Chastity from his fenced-in pasture, he started running in circles like he'd gone crazy. Grandma said he must've been getting senile. Bob died a few months later; we didn't know whether it was from being replaced by Chastity, from old age, or from that stifling Alabama heat.

The peaches and plums had to be gleaned so Grandma could make homemade jellies and preserves. Unlike quilting, there was absolutely no fun in picking fruits and vegetables. The end result was always the same: Grandma gave away most of it, and after Grandpa killed off what was left, we wouldn't have anything to show for all our hard work. At least with quilting you could see the end result.

I'd been in the country for almost nine years. Everything proceeded along a predictable schedule, according to seasonal rhythms. It was as natural as breathing. Every night we'd sit in the dark on the front porch, with two lanterns giving off light. We would sit for hours- me in my swing and Grandma and Grandpa in their rockers. Grandpa ate his "nine o'clocker," as he called it. It consisted of crumpled up day-old cornbread and buttermilk inside a large Mason jar. This was our nightly ritual and I couldn't imagine things being any other way.

Grandma was getting up in age, but still stood straight as an arrow; not even a little bend in her back. She had begun to slow down in small ways. One day when she was out in the fields and I was kneeling in the front yard picking up wood chips for the wood stove, I glanced up to look for her reassuring shape. I knew she was out there, but I couldn't see her. That was odd. I stood up, and looked again. Then I saw her lying motionless in the field. I was off like a bullet shot out of a gun.

She was lying in the dirt, completely still. I screamed; nothing came out of my mouth but air. I shook her but there was no response. I called her name over and over. No answer. I felt her body; it was twice as hot as the air outside. I grabbed hold of her and dragged her limp body across the potato field to the shade of the persimmon tree. A weak moan came out of her mouth. Oh, thank God! I propped her up under the tree, ran as fast as I could to the well, and dipped a bucket of cool water. It felt like it took forever for that bucket to reach the bottom and for me to pull it up from the depths of that deep pit. I begged that old rusty chain not to come off its track like it usually did. Please, not today! With one swift action I poured the water into the Mason jar and ran back through the field to where I'd left Grandma leaning against the tree.

Poor Grandma's shiny black skin turned ashen. Her hands were trembling as I placed the jar onto her lips. She gulped that water down so loud I'd bet you could hear her all the way over at Bethel Hill Elementary School, which was three miles away. It was gone in no time flat. She motioned toward the green weeds with red roots that were scattered around the tree. I pulled up armfuls and gave them to her. She pulled the grassy part away from the roots and sucked on the stems, dirt and all. Then she tossed the used ones aside and did the same thing with the next one. She told me to pull up more. I'd have pulled up that persimmon tree if I had to. She finished off every last one, gaining more and more strength as she drew from those roots.

As soon as I saw that she was okay, I started crying one of those cries that are impossible to control, that go deep in your throat, whimpering and hiccupping. Grandma looked at me with those blue-gray eyes and the light inside them danced like they did the first time I ever laid my eyes on her. She leaned into that tree like she hadn't a care in the world. "Chile, you can really cry; like a great big ol' fountain!" I managed a weak, but relieved, smile. I helped Grandma up and led her into the house.

When Grandma's sons came to visit a couple of weeks later, Uncle Guicy and his brothers were mighty perturbed by what had happened. They got together and decided that an eighty-two year old woman had no business toiling in the fields, especially in that heat. Grandma was going to have to quit farming. No more plowing, tilling, sowing or reaping. No more crops. They told her of their decision and Grandma wasn't about to have any of that. She scoffed at them saying she'd just had a "spell." She'd been working those fields her whole life and she wasn't about to stop now. And that was final. Then she left the room.

The uncles trailed along behind her. They sat her down for a serious talk. They said they were worried about her health and if she refused to see the reason why, then they'd just have to stay there and *keep* her from going out. Grandma's shoulders slumped.

She was outnumbered. A sad look came over her. She went out and sat in the rocker on the front porch, and there she stayed, for days.

Her eyes were dull and she moved around listlessly. I was sure she was permanently depressed and that she'd never be the same old energetic, joyous Grandma, but before too long, she roused herself and started getting back into a routine. She still wasn't the same, but I realized that with time, her inner strength would assert itself.

It was getting on toward six in the evening. Grandpa would be making his slow walk to the front room to turn on the evening news. Grandma was finishing up the supper dishes, and I'd just finished my chore of taking the leftovers out in the yard for the chickens. I wondered about the four o'clock flowers; they were open, but weren't as fully bloomed as they normally were around that time of day. Then I heard the engine of an automobile, far off up the road. There were so many dips and curves in the road that led to the house, the driver usually blew the horn as they rounded the curves to make sure the road was clear.

The sound of the car got closer, and before long, I could see the outline of the old black Buick that belonged to my uncle Guicy. There were several people in the car with him. It pulled up in front of the house. Three men and a woman got out laughing and talking like they'd known each other for years. I was super excited and ran in to tell Grandma that we had company. She was as puzzled as I was about the guests, but when she saw who it was, her arms flung open wide as a meadow, hugging each one of them.

Grandma said, "Go on, chile, give your mama a hug." I almost fell flat on my face. I stood there frozen. My mother turned away, and she and Grandma disappeared into the house. Uncle Guicy leaned over and said he'd miss me, but he'd come to Detroit to visit me whenever he was in the area. I looked at him like he was crazy and thought to myself, "Uncle Guicy sure is confused."

Grandma appeared behind the screen door. The way the sun was shining, all I could see was her silhouette. She stood there for a minute then turned away. I knew something was terribly wrong. I saw my mother come out the front door. I felt like I was having one of those strange dreams you have when a fever strikes in the middle of the night. She took me inside to the room I'd slept in for the past eight years. Without any preamble, she told me to grab my things because she was taking me back to Detroit.

You may well have rolled a bulldozer over me. My face must have turned white because all the blood rushed to the bottom of my stomach. I screamed at the top of my lungs and ran out of the room to find Grandma. I ran from room to room, but she wasn't there. She wasn't anywhere. I went out to the back yard and found her sitting on the old log that she used for chopping the heads off chickens.

I ran up to her like I'd just seen a ghost. "Grandma, Grandma, I won't do it anymore; I promise to be good," I repeated, crying and shaking. Grandma was crying as hard as I was. That let me know this was for real, and not a dream or a silly joke that someone was playing on me. Grandma wiped her eyes with her apron, sat up straight, and said to me, "Wipe your face, chile." She hugged me so hard I thought I might break. "Don' you cry, chile, trouble don' las' always."

I'd heard my Grandparents use this phrase over a hundred times since I came to live with them. For some reason, it impacted me more this time than all the others. We went inside to the front room and she opened the chifferobe. She took out a small gold-colored box. Inside was a pure white handkerchief, which she slowly unfolded and placed in my pocket. Then she gave me two silver dollar coins.

There was worse to come. My mother decreed that my quilt would take up too much space on the long bus ride back to Detroit, and that I couldn't bring it with me. I begged and cried, but she wouldn't relent. Uncle Guicy backed her up. Everything was moving so quickly. We got into the car to leave. My insides were crying, "NO," but I couldn't hold up the flow of events. Uncle Guicy started up the car and I couldn't bear to look at Grandma's face, or Grandpa's. He looked like he wanted to cry, and that was very un-Grandpa like.

The car pulled away as I was being ripped away from the only love I'd ever known. I disintegrated into the leather seats of that Buick as I flashed back to when I first arrived in that big car with those big people. How fitting that it ended just the way it began.

I felt like I'd lost everything. My life was over. As I watched the pine trees go by, I made up my mind that I would never, ever be happy again. I'd put up a shield so no one could hurt me. I'd make sure that no one even got close.

Looking For Me
A small child caught up in a web of turbulence
Then the soft rains came
And with one swat from the warm breeze
I am wisped away to a land of 4 o'clock flowers
And tall oaks
The sun is bright as I go free falling
Down the large grassy grove
My landing is broken by the appearance of
Soft white cotton
Eyes shut tight, yet still can see
The red, green yellow and orange twill
Life takes shape especially after
The appearance of dark chocolate
And all that it represents
My dreams are finally approaching my reality
Suddenly the chocolate completely melts
The four o'clock flower refused to bloom
At their appointed time
The warm rain became a horrible storm
The cotton turned soggy and
All the beautiful colors that I had witnessed
Faded into a balmy blue
The sun disappeared
Dark clouds returned
Completely torn away
And again
I no longer see me

-Phyllis Lawson

CHAPTER 20

LOST IN DETROIT

There wasn't much conversation between my mother and me during that long bus ride from Alabama. All those years of not remembering my mother's face, even with her brief visit to Grandma's, I got a good, long look at it while we traveled together. She had a lot of Grandpa's features: sharp nose and bronze skin, and the tall Horn physique.

I turned away from her and looked out the window. The landscape gradually changed from countryside to small towns to industrial fringes, until we finally came into the lifeless gray of the big city.

When the Greyhound pulled into the bus station in Detroit, my father was there to meet us. He was tall and handsome, with a little mustache. He looked me over and motioned me to the backseat of the car. He didn't say a word then, or on the entire ride through town. I learned that his function in the family was to work, come home, flop in his recliner chair with the newspaper, and whistle. That was it.

We lived in a white frame house at 12673 Turner Street, in Northwest Detroit, in an ethnically diverse neighborhood. I didn't know it at the time, but that part of town was home to many Motown singers. The house was spacious with a big yard, though nowhere near as big as Grandma and Grandpa's farm. There were no four o'clock flowers; just some small beds of straggly yellow and red flowers struggling to bloom. Just like me.

I climbed up to the front door behind my parents feeling heavier with each step. The door opened and a roomful of faces were ogling me. There were so many kids, I thought the neighbors' children were there, but it turned out that they were all my brothers and sisters. Walking in the front door, I struggled to remember the days before I left for Alabama. Seeing my sisters and brothers brought back empty memories. Only their faces and voices were vaguely familiar. As I looked into the eyes of my estranged older sister, all I remembered were the pink ribbons that drooped from my half braided hair on that day I got taken away.

There were no introductions; I was just thrown into the fire. The most surreal thing was coming face to face with my twin brother. I knew I had a twin, but seeing him was like looking into a full-length mirror. I was the girl version of that boy slam banged into a strange new world.

Everything was modern. There was a porcelain tub instead of the huge aluminum one I was accustomed to. They used electric lights instead of kerosene lanterns. I went from sleeping in a bed by myself, to sleeping in a bed with my sisters. I was a complete country hick amidst a city full of familial strangers. For months I'd get up in the night looking for the slop jar, only to snap back into this awful dream.

My brothers took the lead in my orientation process; their teaching method was ridiculous. When I said, "peanut butter and jelly," they howled with laughter at my long country drawl. They said, "You hold those words so long, we could take an hour nap, come back, and they will still be making their way out of your mouth!" They called me "country cornflakes," and I inherited my older sister's jingle, which went like this:

D -A -Double R- K
D – O - G
Spells Darky Dog

They'd keep singing that song along with the "country cornflakes" tag until I'd bust out crying. I was scalded by the mockery and started to keep my mouth shut. I kept my head down and never looked anyone in the eye. I missed Grandma and I'd lie in bed awake at night and long for the comfort and familiarity of my quilt.

I vowed to make myself impervious, but wasn't prepared for a brutal assault like that. It wasn't because they hated me. It was just brothers and sisters ribbing each other. You had to learn to take up for yourself and find a comeback. If you were able to fire back a nice one liner, you won the round and they let you off the hook. That was how they played. It was a good way to prepare me for the tough world on the streets.

There was a pecking order in my family, based on a color scheme: my twin brother was pitch black; my other brother was coal black; there were three light-skinned children and my oldest sister was dark brown. She'd been sent away, like me, to live with our aunt and uncle. Unlike me, she was only there about a year.

Eventually I began to adjust. One day my brothers asked me if I wanted to go to the "party store." I didn't know what that was, but it sounded good to me, so I tagged along. When I got inside, my sweet tooth went Bing! The place was full of what they called "penny candy" – every kind of candy you could ever want. They had every flavored soda pop under the sun. It was a far cry from Millen's. I walked around with my eyes bulging out as my brothers enjoyed my reaction. They bought me a fudgesicle and a bag of potato chips. We sat outside on the steps trying to catch every last drop of ice cream as it dripped down the stick.

I discovered some good things about having siblings. My brothers taught me how to navigate my way around the neighborhood; who were the bullies and who were okay; and where were the best spots to hide out. My oldest sister was a ray of light. She took on the role of trying to be a guide for me. She was the prettiest girl I ever saw with milk chocolate skin, pearly white teeth, and a shape like a soda bottle. She taught me how to dress. The first thing she did was throw away every article of clothing I brought from Alabama - matter of fact, she burned them. No kidding.

My parents were always gone; they worked ALL the time. My father worked as a welder, making automobile parts in a non air-conditioned factory, eight to ten hours a day. Then he did janitorial work at night and on the weekends. My mother worked five days a week in the local school cafeteria. On weekends she worked as a domestic. I felt like she regretted being gone all the time, repeating the same pattern as her mother, but she had to do it in order to help provide for her family.

My mother was an enigma. She had a soft, loving side –gentle as a lamb and fun to be around. And then, from out of nowhere, she'd fly off the handle into a vicious rage. There was no telling when the fury would erupt; she'd be calm for weeks. And then, as if taken over by some evil force, she'd beat me black and blue.

My mother had a story of a dream deferred. She took over the parenting duties for her younger siblings after my Aunt Sarah ran away. After attending Bethel Hill, she went on to Sumter County Training School, the local high school for Black students. She received all "A's" and was on the honor roll every year. She excelled academically and graduated from high school a year early.

She went to Alabama Teachers College at the age of sixteen, got her teaching certificate and taught at Bethel Hill Elementary. She met my father while attending College. He'd run off a year earlier and joined the Navy. He was smitten with her and promised to marry her that following year after his discharge. In the meantime, he was fighting in World War II in the battle of Normandy. When he returned from the war, sure enough, he kept his word and married my mother. After taking their vows, they moved to Detroit.

She never taught in another school. Her two-year teaching certificate didn't meet the criteria in the State of Michigan. Her dream of
being a teacher was shattered. She was a good woman who got caught
up in what most women got caught up in: getting married and having
a slew of children. She couldn't escape from not being able to control
her own destiny because of societal demands. It was a woman's role to
follow the herd.

My mother was intelligent, but instead of using her skills as an edu-
cator, she became a housemaid for White families, just like Grandma.
The hostility and frustration of not being able to fulfill her lifelong
ambitions caused all that bitterness inside her. The constant bearing,
birthing and raising babies, no doubt, contributed to her anger. This
would manifest itself in constant physical and verbal abuse on a weak
target. Me.

She used the belt and the "cat o' nine tails," which was her pet name
for the extension cord. I blamed myself for her viciousness. I desperately tried to find the voice that could tell my mother it was *my* fault
she had to send me away. I thought if I could project the blame onto
myself, it would ease her guilt. If I could just do that, maybe she'd stop
beating me; maybe she'd soften, even if it were only around the edges. I
searched far and wide inside myself for that voice, but I couldn't find it.
I continually bore bruises and visible scars from her rages.

I t was summer, so I had free time until school started in September.
Kids spent their days going out and playing in the streets. From the
way all the neighborhood kids acted, you'd have thought I was from
Mars. They barraged me with unending questions: where did I come
from? Why did I leave there? Why did I talk so funny? They stared at

me like I was a freak of nature; just waiting for me to do some freakish thing they could harp on me about. I started to feel like I was from another planet.

Then I made a friend. Her name was Sandy and she lived in a big green house across the street. She was tall and skinny like me, and just like me, she had two younger brothers who were a pain in the ass. We'd play marathon hide and seek games with all the kids in the neighborhood. Sandy's youngest brother, Fadaryl trailed along behind us, picking his nose. We'd take off running, trying to get away from him and he'd cry so hard, snot would drip down his whole face. Sandy would start feeling sorry for him and stop playing until he felt better. Once he did, he'd run after us with his finger up his nose again, picking away. Like I said, pain in the ass younger brothers.

Sandy and I played together all the time, running around and whispering secrets. Being around her was fun and a little bit of light started returning to my tattered soul.

Then Sandy and her family moved away. It tore a piece out of me that was just beginning to mend. I should have known better to think I'd have something for my own; everything was always taken away from me. Bitterness settled into my heart.

School started in the fall. Mumford High School was the only blue school in Detroit and probably the world; and I mean BLUE! It was painted baby blue inside and out. It was hard on the eyes and worse on your frame of mind. It was three floors tall and I felt like it could bend right over and swallow me whole. There I was, going to High School. It was different from how I dreamed it would be. Instead of feeling like I'd have a wonderful future doing amazing things like Miss Clay said, I was consumed with dread.

When I walked into the swarm of kids in the corridors, I completely shut down. It was like I was sleepwalking. I went into class and just sat there like a zombie, not hearing a word the teachers said. I was in a thick fog that wouldn't lift. Gunshots could be heard in and around the school at least once a week, and gang warfare was a way of life for many of the kids. I knew that I was numb, but couldn't do anything about it. There was nowhere I could go for solace; home was worse than school. I missed Grandma and Grandpa and living in the country, far away from the shithole I was in.

My teachers got frustrated with my inattention and kept sending me to the principal's office. I'd get sent home with a note and get a beating from hell. My body hadn't even healed from the last time my mother flew into one of her rages. They were so frequent it felt like my body became immune to them. I didn't know how to stop myself from sinking into an abyss of despair.

I fell in with a bad crowd, kids who were constantly getting into trouble. Trouble found me wherever I went and sucked me into its vortex. The group I hung with did pills, wine, weed and anything else they could get their hands on. They skipped school and took me right along with them to break into houses and hang out in alleys selling dope. I started getting beatings for skipping school. My mother was increasingly enraged with me. I could count on being beaten as sure as I could count on the sun rising the next day.

I tried getting drunk once. I drank half a bottle of MD 20/20 and that did it for me. Never again. I didn't like the feeling at all. Being that my life was so out of control, I felt like I had to stay *in* control of myself. For lack of having anyone else, I kept hanging out with those kids, but I wasn't drinking or smoking. I became a master of perfecting methods to feign intoxication, just to fit in.

I lost the meaning of everything and couldn't see past the next day. There I was, a kid who used to daydream about the future and what it held for me. I had goals I wanted to achieve. Somehow all those dreams stayed behind, buried in the backyard of my grandparents' farm. They were buried so deep even those mangy chickens couldn't unearth them.

It took everything I had just to get through the day. If there wasn't going to be a tomorrow, I couldn't have cared less.

Then one day I was sitting alone in my room. Out of nowhere, Grandma and every soul I'd encountered in Livingston, gathered inside my head. They surrounded me and talked some sense into me. They told me I needed to remember who I was and where I came from. I needed to remember what was important in life. Then they faded away. I heard that phrase of Grandma and Grandpa's echoing in my head: "Trouble don' las' always, chile."

I came out of that daydream and felt changed. Not that I became suddenly wise and mature, but I knew, with deep certainty, that the life I'd been living: lying, stealing, hanging around with a dead-end crowd, wasn't what I wanted to be doing, and not who I wanted to be. Just like a switch flipped, from that moment on, I quit hanging out with that crowd. I went back to school and showed up every day. I didn't do much of anything in class, but at least I had perfect attendance.

CHAPTER 21

RUNAWAY

B efore too long, I got my first job. It wasn't glamorous, but it paid. It came about through my brothers. Being hardworking boys, they had a newspaper route delivering to over a hundred customers. One of the customers needed someone to clean house three days a week. I jumped all over it with two feet and before you knew it, I was standing on Mrs. Sloan's front porch.

The Sloan's were an elderly Jewish couple. Mr. Sloan owned a grocery business and was gone most of the time. Mrs. Sloan was diabetic and suffered from heart problems, so she stayed home. I felt sorry for her. Her legs were swollen black and blue and looked like elephant limbs. She was in constant pain. Mrs. Sloan was a real pack rat, hoarding things that belonged in the garbage. She hung on to stuff that served no earthly purpose, as if it was a precious treasure. When I cleaned her house, I took newspapers down to the basement and put them in a neat stack next to all the other newspapers that were there. She had newspapers dating back to the 1950's. It was a fire waiting to happen. God forbid someone were to light a match down there.

She was an orthodox Jew so she ate kosher food consisting of roasted eggs, wine matzo, parsley and horseradish. I hated the roasted eggs because she'd eat those half-done eggs, then leave the plates until I came back to wash them. The yellow part was left in the sink coagulating for days and I had a helluva time cleaning it off. It was disgusting. She'd cook cow tongue; that big ugly slab of a thing. She'd boil it in an open pot on the stove and every time I caught sight of it, my stomach turned. I remembered getting nauseous watching Grandpa devour chicken feet. Together, Grandpa and the Sloan's would've made some kind of dinner table!

Mrs. Sloan taught me a lot about Jewish history. She liked to talk about the old country and I listened with interest. She even showed me the numbers on her forearm from the concentration camp. She must've been made of steel to have survived all that. She reminded me of Grandma Lula. They were old, had lots of stories to tell, and they both faced unconscionable hardships. Being at Mrs. Sloan's was a welcomed relief from the hell of my life at home.

She talked me to death while I worked. One day, she showed me an old quilt that had been passed down from her mother. She noticed how sullen I became and asked me what was wrong. I couldn't bring myself to say anything. How could I talk about my quilt, or my grandparents, or growing up in Alabama? It brought back memories of my grandma and our time together, and it made me sad. My grandparents' home was my Camelot and I missed it till I ached. I couldn't bear to reminisce about those times. It would spiral me down into a gaping wound of loss. As it was, I was dying inside already.

Spending time with Mrs. Sloan and going to school was the only solace I had. Mrs. Sloan always asked about my grades and how I was doing in school. I lied to her because I didn't want her to think of me as someone who had no ambition. I told her what I thought she wanted to hear, like how my History class was studying Jewish History and the Holocaust, just to shift the focus off me and back to what she enjoyed talking about. I couldn't bring myself to tell her I was passing my classes by the skin of my teeth. Nor could I tell her the only reason I went to school was to avoid the bad kids who tried luring me into foolishness. I developed the same respect for Mrs. Sloan as I did for Grandma, Aunt Tudney, Miss Sugar and all the other old people I loved and was ripped away from. I often wondered what Aunt Honey Bee would say if she knew that getting a "D" was a huge accomplishment for me.

The teachers eventually passed me on to ninth grade. Not because I had learned anything, but because I think they felt sorry for me. One day, purely by accident, I discovered poetry. I was sitting in my English class, half-listening to the teacher recite a poem we'd been working on all week. When she was done, she asked the class what we thought it meant. The last thing I remembered was my hand shooting up like a rocket that had just been launched. I stood in the front of the room with thirty sets of eyes glued to me like flies on shit. The words came spiraling out into a flow of rhymes that revealed the depth of how I felt about my life.

I fell in love with what came pouring out of me. It was a delayed response to a poem by Langston Hughes called "A Dream Deferred." Our English Lit class had been wearing that poem out while the teacher was worn to the bone trying to squeeze out an interpretation from the class. I knew the poem like the back of my hand, yet all week, I was too scared to admit I had an opinion about it, a deep opinion, for that matter. That poem described my life like it'd been written just for me. It expressed my sorrow, my pain, and above all else, my dreams that seemed to have imploded into a barren field of nothingness.

It was no longer Mr. Hughes' dream that was deferred; it was mine. I blurted out my interpretation of that poem in one beautiful, fluid soliloquy. I was oblivious to my surroundings. I couldn't explain what exactly came out of my mouth that day. It felt like I was channeling something or someone greater than myself, like a spirit of sorts. Maybe it was Aunt Honey Bee, who died a few years back. Maybe it was myself, struck with a wisdom I never knew was inside me.

My teacher was awestruck. I guess she was puzzled that the student who was as quiet as a church mouse, suddenly possessed an ability to give an analysis of a poem that would leave even Mr. Langston Hughes himself, speechless. After the bell rang, all the kids sat there with their jaws dropped like they hung off loose hinges. My teacher said she'd never heard anything like that in all her years of teaching. She encouraged me to write regardless of my home life. She told me not to let it deter me from creating. As I left the room, I felt all those kind spirits that Grandma mentioned that day in the cotton fields. They were standing there with me, helping me put one foot in front of the other as I held my head a little bit higher that day.

I began writing furiously. It was like an open fire hydrant that I couldn't turn off. I was spilling out words like if I didn't get them out, I'd choke to death. I started skipping school to sit on the banks of the Detroit River, writing my most intimate thoughts and turning them into poetry. I couldn't stop. I wrote till my hand hurt. I wrote until my heart stopped hurting so much.

Trouble came along innocently enough. It came in the form of Benson and Hedges non-menthol cigarettes, which Mr. Sloan left lying around on the coffee table. It was too tempting; I had to light one up. With the first hit, I thought I was going to throw up. It was worse than my grandparents' snuff. I thought of Grandma Lula shaking her head and saying I was "tryin' to be grown."

I continued pilfering the cigarettes until I learned how to smoke without coughing my lungs out. Mr. Sloan caught on, so I started buying my own. There were only two kinds of cigarettes that most Black people smoked: Kools or Newports; I chose Kool Milds.

As soon as I started smoking, my mother smelled it on me and flew into a blind rage. She beat me to a pulp. I came up with all kinds of smoke-removing tactics, thinking I could fool her. My main tactic was to avoid her as much as possible.

A couple of weeks later, she came home unexpectedly for a lunch break. There I was, reeking of cigarette smoke. She looked at me in a fury. She said this time she'd be giving me a 'whupping' I'd never forget. As if I forgot *any* of them. She told me I better be ready when she got off work. The timing couldn't have been worse. When she got home, she saw my progress report from school with the lowest marks I'd ever gotten. She told me to brace myself because she was going to pound me senseless. I went to my room and sat on the bed. I sat there numb as a lump for half an hour. Suddenly, I jerked up and started pacing back and forth with my mind spinning circles. When I thought about the prospect of another beating, something shifted inside me. All details fell away and the only thing I knew for sure was: I'd had enough.

Fear shot through me like a bolt of lightning. You know you're scared when the spit dries up in your mouth. I realized that it was decision time and I had to move quickly. I grabbed stuff from the drawer, not in any order, just grabbing and shaking with my heart pounding like a jackhammer inside my chest. The next thing I knew, I was flying out the side door of my parents' house. I didn't look back. I don't remember hearing the door slamming behind me. I just ran. I ran like demons were chasing me.

Without thinking, I ended up at Mrs. Sloan's house. Luckily I was able to open the side door that led to her basement. I stretched out across the stacks of newspapers lined up against the back wall and closed my eyes. I was so overwrought and full of adrenaline, I couldn't even cry. It was cold and damp. I balled up like a fetus, pulled my old wool coat over my head and tried to sleep.

I heard the sound of feet. It was Mrs. Sloan's snail pace entering the kitchen just above the basement. My whole body tensed up. I was terrified she'd come downstairs. She clanked and clattered pots and pans until eventually, it was clear she wasn't coming down. Then I remembered she *never* came down to the basement since I did all the washing and ironing and her legs weren't able to carry her up and down the wooden steps. There was no way she'd suspect I was there. I'd just show up on her doorstep for work at my regular times and she'd never know I was hiding out.

It worked perfectly. I was hyper-careful not to make any noise or turn on lights. I made sure if I ran the water in the sink, I'd do it simultaneously with when the furnace turned on so it'd drown out the noise of the water. Once I heard one of the Sloan's in the kitchen and the door to the basement was open. I panicked. Fortunately, they didn't come downstairs. The Sloan's never suspected me of being a stowaway.

As far as I knew, my mother never looked for me or reported me missing. I guess she was glad I was gone. The stimulation of my daring escape and the fear of detection lasted for a couple of weeks. After that wore off, my life felt even drearier than it did before. There I was, sleeping on a pile of newspapers in a dark, dank basement. I had no place to go and nothing to look forward to.

I didn't want to go to school; it seemed pointless. I couldn't get in touch with my sisters, figuring that would cause dissension between them and my parents. I didn't even have the energy to get up from the piles of newspapers and go for a walk. I felt a diffuse pain that never let up. I told myself I was worthless. I found myself thinking about ways to die. If only I could think of a quick, painless way to end it all, my problems would evaporate.

One night I was lying on my newspaper bed, sunk in despair, when I heard words from somewhere deep in my head, "…Yea, though I walk through the valley of the shadow of death, I will fear no evil; for thou art with me; thy rod and thy staff, they comfort me."

A rush of warmth slid through my skin and into my bones. The Twenty-Third Psalm! Grandma used to recite it to me every night. Tears squeezed into my eyes as I mumbled the words, "The Lord is my shepherd..." As I spoke those words with tears streaming down my face, I felt a lift in my soul. I started thinking about how all those folks down south who prayed, and Grandma who often spoke of the power of prayer, were definitely onto something.

After that, I repeated the Twenty-Third Psalm every night and threw in the Lord's Prayer for good measure. I came to feel there was a power much larger than myself that wanted me to live. It wanted to live through me. I remembered how Grandma told me she thought I possessed an old spirit. She said I reminded her of Ella. I knew how enamored Grandma was by Ella's strength and perseverance. The fact that I reminded her of Ella brought some life back into my weary bones.

Gradually, I felt more like a real person. My energy returned and I went for walks around the city during the day. I'd go past the public library, and pretty soon, I started going in. I discovered an enormous hunger for the books in there. I wanted to read everything from Plato and Socrates to Black History. I soaked up every kind of knowledge. Something in my brain kicked into gear and I found myself restless in a way I couldn't identify. I daydreamed and fantasized wildly. I felt determined to do *something*.

I decided to go to Pittsburg. I don't know why I chose Pittsburg, unless it was because of a picture in a magazine I saw where cobblestone streets looked pristine and inviting. I bought a one-way Greyhound bus ticket. I wanted to say goodbye to Mr. and Mrs. Sloan, but I realized I couldn't do that. I couldn't tell anyone. The last thing I wanted was for someone to come fetch me.

There I was fifteen years old, on the road, with little money and nowhere to go. For the first time in my life, I'd sprouted myself some wings. I looked out the window at the small rural towns going by and realized, even they were part of my past now. Once again, I was heading down an unknown road, but this time was different. I was the one in control of my uncharted destiny. I may not have known where I was headed or what lay in store for me, but at that moment, I didn't need to know.

CHAPTER 22

HOMELESS

The Pittsburgh Bus Terminal was full of people, travelers milling around in every direction, filling up the waiting areas. Buses pulled in and out of the station all night long, going to Lord knows where. On the fringes were the homeless people with everything they owned either tied to their bodies or in broken-down grocery baskets.

I scouted around for a place to spend the night. I wasn't the only one scrounging for a place to rest. In the bathroom, a couple of older women camped out; they looked like seasoned veterans. I settled down on the floor next to them. Women and girls of all ages came in and out like a revolving door, chattering and flushing. When the hour got late, the only people left were us transients. We didn't speak to each other. The whole time I was there, we never spoke a word. I wondered if that was some unwritten code of homelessness.

The woman next to me looked battle-scarred. She was covered with bruises and when she took off her shoes, it looked like someone had beaten her feet with a lead pipe. They were swollen black and blue. She reminded me of all the women Grandma told me about: Ella, Cooter, Miss Daisy and all the others. It was a different century, but the same old story.

I was happy being in a new place, a million miles from the ferocious hands of my mother. I was full of energy. I roamed the streets during the day and spent nights in the bus terminal or other places that stayed open all night, like hospitals. It never occurred to me to be afraid. I was in survival mode. The days were long so I wandered around looking for discarded food or for somewhere to rest my feet. Then I found a library. That was the perfect place to spend my time. I could read all day, stay put, and pass my time in the endless stories of people who cared enough to write them down.

I came up with the bright idea of getting myself locked inside at night. When everyone had gone home, I had the whole place to myself. I discovered a refrigerator with food in it! I tore into it like a rabid animal. I went into the bathroom and gave myself a sink bath. Oh, Lord! Clean and well fed in a building full of books. I was in heaven. The next morning, I blended right in with the folks just coming in, and life in the library went on as usual. I decided it was best not to push my luck, so I moved on to one of the other libraries in the city.

Avoiding the cops was a big concern. I was nervous, constantly on the lookout for those blue uniforms. I knew my luck had to run out sooner or later and that one day, I'd look up to see them coming to haul me away to God knows where. I'd rather be sleeping on the bathroom floor of that train station with the ladies who never said a word. My senses were heightened and I was on alert.

Being a transient was like being in school. I had to study how others survived. I watched panhandlers beg in front of a restaurant and figured I could put my hand out and tell hard-luck stories, too. Turns out I had more stories to tell about my misfortunes than the libraries had books. I'd walk up to strangers with my 'woe is me' face and tell a sob story about not being able to get home because I lost my bus fare. I put my little Southern accent on thick and watched how easy it was to prey on peoples' sympathy. I got pretty brazen with my story telling, milking that southern drawl with all I had. I made up lots of stories and got myself a shitload of money doing it.

One night, my conscience got the best of me in the form of Grandma's voice. I started thinking about how disappointed Grandma would be for carrying on like this. Grandma warned me as a child to not take food from strangers. She insisted I say "No thank you, ma'am" or "No thank you, Sir." This was a chilling thought and my begging life came to an abrupt halt. I resorted to dumpster-diving and petty thievery instead.

I was constantly on edge and grew more paranoid with every passing day. I had nightmares about blue uniforms. One night, I came back to the bus station with an exhaustion that made my legs buckle. I found a spot in the women's bathroom, slid down the wall to the floor and immediately fell asleep. The next thing I knew, a tall White woman was hovering over me saying, "Your name and age please. Let me see your ID."

I couldn't do anything but confess that I was a runaway.

It was just like my nightmares where the cops in blue uniforms came and yanked me away to Juvenile Hall. In a way, I felt relieved to have it over. It had been over six months since the last time I had a good night's sleep or a warm plate of food.

Unfortunately, the main dish served in "Juvie," as us kids called it, was cake bologna.

I ate so much of that crap that I began to smell like it. I guess it was better than dumpster- diving and disappointing Grandma by accepting food from strangers.

There I was, locked up with all the other young troublemakers of the world. I had nowhere to go and couldn't go back home. This was a problem for the social workers so they made me a ward of the court. I was sent to a shelter for young girls back in Detroit. They didn't know what else to do with me.

The shelter was a hellhole and I knew it from the minute I walked in the front door. Two girls were beating the crap out of each other while two residential counselors sat there and ate their lunches, blabbering away. At one point during the ruckus, one of the girl's earrings flew onto the lunch table right in front of the counselors. They looked at each other, laughed, and continued talking like nothing at all had occurred.

Mrs. Stack, who probably stood all of four feet five inches, with an ass just as wide, ushered me to the door and sarcastically announced, "You see these doors? No locks, no keys; so any time you want to leave, you don't have to run away, you can walk." And that's exactly what I did. When my bed was found empty the next morning, I guarantee no one blinked an eye in that dumping ground for misplaced, misguided, and forgotten kids.

There I was again, on the street, right back where I started over six months ago. It was deflating. I wasn't even sixteen yet, so I had limited options. I wanted to call my sisters so badly, but again, I didn't want to put them in a bad position with my mother by helping me. I reluctantly gave up on that idea. Then I did the simplest thing I could think of: I went down to Detroit Police Headquarters at 1300 Beaubien Street, found a quiet corner right outside their front steps, curled up in a ball and went to sleep. It didn't take long for someone to find me right there outside the door of the law.

That strategy turned out to be beneficial. I met Officer Joanne Post, who saved my life. She was in the Runaway Division and took over my case. She was the whitest woman I'd ever seen; outspoken, crisp and direct. She reminded me of Ruby Tartt, but gentle and caring. When she took me into the police station, I sat in her office and my whole story came pouring out: growing up on a farm, my grandma, the quilt, Mrs. Sloan, my mother and running away from home. She was a good listener and had a compassionate heart.

I was adamant about never going back to any shelter, or anyplace that faintly resembled one. I asked if I could be sent back to Livingston to live with my grandparents. There was no easy answer. She took me home with her to where she lived with her mother. She could've been fired for taking in a poor Black girl from inner city Detroit. She fed me, spent time with me and talked sense into me. Being at Officer Post's home gave me a sense of security and warmth that I hadn't felt for a long time. I didn't know why she decided to become my mentor, but I knew I'd be forever grateful to her for going over and above the call of duty.

She set up a meeting with my mother in order to try to re-establish communication between us. The three of us sat there rigidly at the kitchen table of the house I ran away from: me, my mother; and Officer Post, my only ally in this fight. When she broached the subject of me returning to Alabama to live with my grandparents, my mother leaned in, her eyes flashing, and said, "Not if hell freezes over! That girl will never, ever, set foot in Livingston again, not over my dead body!" Officer Post drew back in surprise, then tried to steer the subject around to something my mother would find agreeable. My mother wouldn't yield an inch. That meeting turned out to be brief.

Luckily, I turned sixteen in September, and with the help of Officer Post, I was able to enter the Cleveland Job Corps Center for Women. That institution was a saving grace that housed, trained, and educated over three hundred girls between sixteen and twenty-one years old. I would be there for the next two years.

CHAPTER 23

A New Road

The Cleveland Job Corps Center for Women prepared girls to become women, socially, emotionally and economically. It was also a place made up of girls from all over the United States who needed to gain occupational skills. A young lady could complete her high school education through a joint partnership with the local high school. They sweetened the pot with a nice little stipend that gave us an incentive to finish.

I fit right in. I needed to make up for lost time and was ready to get on with my life. I had two roommates, and the three of us became good friends. We all had similar backgrounds. Suzanne was a small-framed girl with a quick wit who liked to crack jokes about her mother who had abused her. Her mom's boyfriend tried to molest her and her mother blamed her for it. She got kicked out of the house when she was only fifteen. She roamed around Cleveland, living on the streets and with friends until she ended up at Job Corps.

Patricia Barnett was a shy, quiet girl from Chicago. She had to be the saddest person I ever met. Her mother was an alcoholic and drug addict who beat Tricia unmercifully when she couldn't get her fix. Tricia left home a few months before the police raided her house. We shared bunk beds and at night I'd hear her crying under the covers.

The three of us spent most of our time together. Suzanne and I always tried to make Tricia laugh, but she never managed more than a half-smile. We made a pact that we'd all achieve greatness, and whoever fell, we'd lift them up and carry them the rest of the way.

I never finished high school and needed remediation for the years I'd been mentally absent in school. I was strong in English and Spelling, but Science, Math and American History were a completely different story. I had a lot of catching-up to do. And I *hated* Math. There was no way around it; I had to do the dirty work: sit down, listen to the teacher, then go home and study. It wasn't fun and it wasn't easy. I plowed my way through it. Some of the other kids told me I'd never make it because I wasn't smart enough. The difficulties seemed insurmountable.

My tough-nosed counselor, Mr. Fagan, didn't take any nonsense and was forever riding my tail to achieve. His favorite words to me were, "Get your butt off the pity pot and get on the success train." I'd think about the story Grandma told me about Ella's ability to continue to get up and stand toe to toe with her enemy, even after being struck by a hot iron. That story gave me the courage to continue.

Very rarely did a day go by that I didn't think about Grandma, and no matter how hard I tried to forget, the quilt always found its way into my consciousness. It wasn't all about the quilt itself, but the stories inside it. All those souls…it seemed like I was a link to them, like I had to keep going in order to keep them going. I thought of all the people who had come before me. The only way my history would be preserved was for me to be strong and not allow my painful past to become a detriment to my future. I was the torchbearer for the souls embedded in those used pieces of cloth.

I wrote a lot of poetry during the two years at the Job Corps Center. I filled up an entire hardcover diary with poems. I never shared my poetry with anyone, but decided one day to read some poems to Suzanne and Tricia. I was self-conscious when I started, but could see from their reaction that they understood what the poems meant. What they said to me was right: that somehow all the bad stuff sounded better when it was transformed into a poem. I told Tricia I would write a poem about her and it would be a "happy poem with a beautiful ending." That was the only time I saw Patricia smile without covering her mouth like she was ashamed.

It took two years, but I did it. I completed the program. On graduation day, I walked across the stage with my High School Diploma in one hand and a certificate as a secretary in the other. I felt a sense of accomplishment; something solid I could be proud of myself for. Suzanne was in the audience whooping and hollering. I looked around for Tricia and couldn't understand why she wasn't there. I had proved to myself, and to the world, that I was not going to let life defeat me. I had learned from my mistakes, left my past behind, and was starting out fresh with a Job Corp certificate in my back pocket.

After graduation, and our celebration, Suzanne and I went back up to our dorm. When we opened the door, Mr. Fagan, the counselor, was waiting there with a serious look on his face. I had a terrible feeling. He told us Tricia hung herself. She was found dangling from the ceiling in the laundry room. Suzanne started shrieking and crying hysterically, but it sounded like it came from the other end of a long tunnel. I felt like I was going to pass out. I collapsed to the floor trying to wrap my head around it all and kept thinking I let her down somehow.

What happened to the pact we made about not letting the others fall down? What went through her mind when she wrapped that rag around her neck? Suzanne and I were busy celebrating my personal achievement while Tricia was seeing no way out other than to take herself out completely. I didn't know how I was ever going to forgive myself.

Later that day, I gathered up my broken, grieving self and went to the Cleveland Riverfront. I realized I had to get out of this place.

I took out my diary, ripped out all the pages and threw them in the water. I watched them float away down the river like they were fallen leaves from trees up above. From that moment on, everything was different.

CHAPTER 24

INTO THE BLUE

To get into the military, all I had to do was pass the Armed Forces entrance exam. It wasn't as easy as I thought. A lot of people wanted to join. Most of the young women I knew from Job Corps were signing up for it and the test was *hard*. With my new high school diploma, I jumped on the bus and hopped over to the Armed Forces Recruiting Center on Euclid Avenue. The recruiters' eyes lit up when I came through the door. Army and Air Force vied with each other to gain my interest. I liked the idea of flying and the Air Force's pretty blue suits didn't hurt any. I filled out mounds of paperwork and was put on the list to take the test. That was my first step.

On the day of the test, my confidence took a dive. What was I doing? I was sure to fail miserably. There I was, sitting in a large open room with fifty other would-be recruits, all of them a million times smarter than me. I wanted to jump up and run out of that room. I ended up sitting on my hands. Even though it was eighty degrees inside, my fingers were ice-cold from fear.

A baby-faced Sergeant appeared in the front of the room barking off orders like Miss Sugar: "Pick the pencil up, put the pencil down, stop, go, stand up, sit down, leave the room, don't leave the room," and on and on. Nobody took their eyes off this loud- mouthed, baby-faced man until he finished putting more fear into our hearts than what was already there. Then he gave the signal to pick up our pencils and begin.

There were twenty different tests — no kidding - and it took six hours to complete all of them. It seemed like four lifetimes that we sat there sweating it out in one spot. The further along I went, the worse I felt about my chances. My brain and my fingers went numb.

Finally it was over. What a relief! We turned in the tests and were directed down the hallway where the men and women were separated. The women were sent to a bathroom where we had to strip down to our undies. We were handed a cup and told to pee in it. My aim must've been piss-poor (no pun intended) because I kept missing the cup. I had to drink water and wait till it ran through me like a stream. There were no drugs in my urine because I was deathly afraid of anything that caused me to lose my sense of self-control. I wasn't pregnant because if I were, it would've been an immaculate conception!

Then came the news from the written test. I had passed! I was ecstatic. After years of being tossed around aimless, I had taken control of my life! I had chosen what I wanted to do and I was right on track! I was floating on a bed of clouds.

I took my first airplane ride when I flew to Lackland Air Force Base, in Texas, for Basic Training. Training consisted of being ordered around constantly for twelve weeks. Every waking minute someone was up in your face telling you what to do, how to do it, when to do it, and man, you better jump to it! I loved it. The other recruits grumbled, but not me. I felt like I belonged. I was proud of myself. It wasn't long before, I'd been struggling just to survive: endless nights of sleeping on floors, eating garbage, feeling despair and discouragement, barely hanging on. But I battled through it.

I was in the Air Force ready to take anything the Drill Sergeants had to dish out. Their verbal tirades were music to my ears. I was fine with peeling every potato in the chow hall or scrounging through every piece of mud on the obstacle course. I already overcame the worst hurdles imaginable and felt like the discipline would only make me better. I sailed through Basic Training.

Then I was given my first assignment: Air Force Technical School. I was going to be an aircraft maintenance technician. I coughed and rolled my eyes inwardly when the Air Force recruiter assured me that I'd love this career field. What he failed to mention was that he had a quota to fill. He needed to place a certain number of women into non-traditional fields. The ink on the directive was still wet with the signature of Richard Nixon.

I didn't balk at messing around with the hydraulic systems of B52 bombers. I studied hard and graduated at the top of my class. I became a qualified Airman First Class in the U.S. Air Force and was assigned to a military base in northern California, dead in the middle of a desert. It was like a dream: living in California, working every day in my beautiful blue uniform, and earning good money. I held my head up and could look people in the eye. That was a genuine measure of just how far I'd come.

My supervisors looked at me as a leader. I spent my days repairing aircraft that sat in large airplane hangars. The temperatures reached 110 degrees during summer months and just surviving that heat was a challenge in and of itself. I listened to my fellow Airmen grumble about being at the worst military base in California, but I was grateful to be there. I understood exactly what Grandma meant when she said, "You nev'r miss your water 'til the well run dry." I couldn't wish for anything more than what I had in that moment.

It was the early 1970's and as the only woman working on B-52's at that time, I lived in a sea of sexist remarks. It didn't matter that I knew more than the men about the mechanics of the aircraft. It bent their egos. My approach to the situation was humor: "Oh, no, would you just look at that! I broke a nail and the polish is chipping off." Or I'd go on about how my uniform always got so messy. I'd ask one of them to explain the difference between a screwdriver and a wrench just to appease them. In response, they'd say, "Oh, sweetheart, let us men take care of this. You can go inside the hanger and fix those pretty little nails of yours." I retained my dignity, but there was no stopping their sexism.

My revenge was subtle. I spent hours in the air-conditioned hanger studying. When it came time to test for the next promotion, I aced it. I was promoted and ended up being their supervisor. You could have knocked them over with a gasket. The Air Force introduced stability into my life. I learned how to negotiate my way through the ranks and became accomplished at a high skill level. These were good general life lessons; plus I got to see a lot of the world. I became a strong, independent, self-assured woman, just like Grandma Lula.

I was a long way away from Grandma and I missed her with every bone in my body. I missed Grandpa, Miss Sugar, Aunt Honey Bee, and all the others back in the country. I even missed my mother and father. With the perspective of my new maturity, I realized they had their problems too. Deep down inside, I cared about them. I guess I was becoming what Grandma referred to as 'grown'. Even though it'd been seven years since seeing her, Grandma would send me letters with a crisp one-dollar bill every year since I'd left. Except for that year- a signal to me that something was wrong.

I was able to get three weeks leave to visit family. I was dying to see the old farm, to take my shoes off and run up that dirt road, just like the old days. I wanted to find my quilt, bring it back to California and never let it out of my sight again.

When the plane landed in Birmingham, I called Aunt Phyllis. I longed to be near Grandma again and felt her presence running through me. Aunt Phyllis answered the phone. I blurted out that I was at the Birmingham airport and needed a ride to Livingston. She could hear the excitement in my voice, but her own voice trailed away. She said slowly, "I thought your mother told you what happened." My heart froze. Fear shot through me like it had so many times over the years.

I told her no one had told me anything. Then she dropped the bomb. It chewed up my insides and spit them out right there on the floor. My grandparent's house had burned to the ground and they had come to live with her in Birmingham. I couldn't respond. Aunt Phyllis kept calling my name. My ears heard her loud and clear, but I couldn't grasp what she was saying. I found myself standing at the phone booth trying to stop time, trying to go back and prevent the house from burning down. I recreated the incident in my mind, and was able to stop it from going up in flames.

The next thing I knew, Aunt Phyllis was in front of the airport. I guess I'd been 'out of my body' wandering around back and forth, crying. I felt like a chicken with its head cut off. People kept coming up to me asking if I was OK. Even a policeman tried to find out what the problem was, thinking I might've been robbed. Aunt Phyllis explained the situation and took me to her car. I sobbed all the way from the airport to the front door of her house.

There was Grandma. She was standing at the front door. I jumped out of the car and ran into her wide-open arms as she wrapped me in a tearful embrace. "Chile, chile, chile, you a sight fo' sore eyes. I sure do love your heart and your liv'r, too." Suddenly everything bad melted away and was right again.

She looked well, considering what she'd gone through. The light in her eyes was as bright as I remembered. I went in to see Grandpa. He looked older from all those years of suffering from rheumatism, arthritis, and asthma. He flashed one of those man-on-the-Kool-Aid-pitcher smiles and gave me a huge hug. He said something in a hushed whisper so I put my ear to his lips to hear him say, "My li'l Black gal." A tear rolled down his face. That was the first time I'd ever seen Grandpa cry.

We gathered in Aunt Phyllis' small kitchen and I fixed Grandpa a bowl of his favorite cold crumbled cornbread and buttermilk. They told me the story of the house burning down. I got chills. It was like one of those old myths where humans are punished for trying to outsmart nature. It started off as a good deed. Grandma's sons decided to go in together and buy Grandma an electric stove because she was getting too old to be cutting and toting wood for her stove every day.

I remembered how I loved getting the modern stuff, like when we first got the television and Grandma succumbed to having it in the big room even though she didn't want or need a modern contraption. Their house was old and not made for electrical wiring. I had watched Grandma feed her old stove with wood or charcoal for years. She didn't want to hurt her sons' feelings or appear ungrateful, so she ended up with a brand new electric stove. I could only imagine how she struggled with trying to learn food preparation on this new-fangled technology. It pained me to think about it.

One night, about a week after installing the new stove, they went to bed as usual. During the middle of the night, Grandma said she woke up and saw the room filling with thick smoke. She didn't think twice. She jumped up and at ninety-plus years old, picked up Grandpa and carried him out of the house. Had he tried to walk by himself, he'd never have made it out. Seeing as how Grandma never would've left him, they both would've perished. When I asked her how on earth she managed to carry him, she replied, "The Lord done help me carry Edgar out the house. Don' nev'r be surprise what the Lord can do, chile."

Cousin Jeff later told Aunt Phyllis that when he arrived at the farm, Grandma had wrapped Grandpa in a quilt. He was shaking like a leaf. Grandma Lula stood by and watched over him all night. The old house caught quickly and the fire blazed up. It was burning out of control way too fast for two old people to do anything about. It made a huge bonfire and could be seen from miles away.

Cousin Jeff saw the smoke and was the first one to arrive on the scene. Aunt Bessie also saw the smoke from her property, a few miles away. She got up, lit her kerosene lantern and high tailed it through the darkness, across the swamp to my grandparents' house. Cousin Jeff's son, Robert also came running to help. They tried to get water from the well to put the fire out, but it was too close to the house and the heat from the fire drove them back. There was nothing they could do but watch the fire burn itself out. I shuddered to think how Grandma and Grandpa suffered in that hour.

Rain came and put the remains of the fire out. By the grace of God, a few things were miraculously spared: Grandma's old cedar chest containing some quilts and keepsakes, the grandfather clock that sat on the mantle, the old churn, and a few pieces of clothes. The "bag of rags," as I used to call them, was consumed by the fire and gone forever. My cherished past had gone up in smoke. I had held the idea of Livingston remaining in my heart as a secret promise that someday I could return to the serenity of my youth. It devastated me to realize that day would never come.

The four o'clock flowers were gone. I'd never hear the rest of the stories inside the cloths of that old cotton sack. All the treasured photographs, the historical artifacts in the chifferobe that Grandma had been collecting for years; her last mementoes of Joe and Emma Young; all the artifacts of her heritage were gone forever. I knew my grandmother was hurting inside even worse than me, but she never showed a trace of it.

It took a lot to gather my nerves to ask Aunt Phyllis about my quilt; I was afraid of what I might hear. I took her aside as not to bother Grandma; she had a huge burden to carry already. Aunt Phyllis said she didn't know. It wasn't in the cedar chest. When they looked inside, there were three quilts, but none of them were mine. She remembered that after the fire, Cousin Jeff took Grandma and Grandpa to his house and maybe my quilt was there. Was my quilt the one Grandma wrapped around Grandpa when she carried him out of the house that night? Did I dare hope? I'd have to wait for the weekend to find out when Aunt Phyllis planned to take me down to the country. She said we'd stop by Cousin Jeff's house to see if it was there. The weekend didn't come fast enough.

I got Aunt Phyllis up early on Saturday morning and hustled us into the car. We drove along the dirt roads that led into the wooded pasturelands, me daydreaming about sitting under that old persimmon tree. Suddenly, I felt the car hitting the bumpy road leading to Cousin Jeff's property line. Before Aunt Phyllis could pull up to the grassy spot in front of his house, I jumped out and was banging on his door like I was the police.

Cousin Jeff's truck was nowhere in sight, which usually meant he was out. I kept pounding as if that would make him magically appear. Aunt Phyllis begged me to stop and told me to get back in the car. She said we'd come back after going to the site of my grandparents' farmhouse. We drove down the hill past the pine trees. I swear I could smell the charred remains of the house. As we pulled up to the front yard, I saw that the only thing remaining was the concrete stoop.

There was no way I could've prepared myself for what I saw. There was a cavernous hole where there should have been a house. Everything I knew and loved had been sucked in and all that was left was a pile of dirty, black rubble. I felt off-balance. Part of my world was missing. I needed to sit down fast. I stumbled over to the stump that Grandma used to sit on in the backyard. I closed my eyes and tried to call up the days when I'd sit with Grandma on that stoop. My mind went blank. Charred like the remains of that big old house that once had so much life in it.

Fragments of dishes and other unrecognizable objects were scattered around. Aunt Phyllis and her brothers combed through it many times, but she patiently waited while I sifted around for about an hour. I didn't know what I was looking for. I guess I was just looking for something, but instead, all I found was nothing.

We were silent all the way back to Cousin Jeff's house. When we got there, his old blue pickup was sitting out front. I bolted out of the car, and climbed into the bed of the truck to see if my quilt was there to be found. All I saw were piles of wood. Cousin Jeff came around the side of the house. He wasn't the most animated man in the world. His facial expression rarely changed from being serious and dignified. I only saw him laugh a couple of times in my life, one of which was when I blundered into the house of the dead man.

There he was, tall and serious, and there I was, in my hyper way, jumping up and down while frantically asking him about the quilt that was wrapped around Grandpa on that fateful night. He looked at me evenly and told me his daughter had taken the quilt home with her to Georgia. When I nearly busted a gut, he calmly said he'd get in touch with her and have it sent to Aunt Phyllis' house. I had no choice but to be content with his answer. He looked at me strangely, but was used to my goings-on. I guess he wasn't surprised that I was still so excitable even though I was a grown woman.

CHAPTER 25

STITCHED WHOLE

In the fall of October 1977, I was stationed in one of the most remote places on earth - the Aleutian Islands, a chain extending westward from Alaska into the Bering Sea. It was the smallest island in the chain, a whopping four miles long and two miles wide; a rock in the middle of icy water, one hundred and sixty miles from Russia where snowstorms constantly assailed the island. It was so tiny and isolated and the weather was so bad that we'd gone without soap and toothpaste for two weeks. We patiently waited for the barge that carried our supplies and food to make its way across the Bering Sea.

I didn't find out that Grandpa died until three days after the event because that's how long Red Cross had been trying to get a telephone call through. He'd become ill and the doctors concluded that he'd had prostate cancer for a long time. Radiation therapy was suggested, but Grandpa adamantly refused. Grandma told the doctors to "jus' let him be."

Aunt Phyllis explained how one morning he'd gotten up from bed and could barely stand. He rejected going to the doctor even though he completely lost his appetite. Two days later, Aunt Phyllis convinced him to go, and even then, he put up a fight. When the doctor asked Grandpa about his symptoms, he wouldn't open his mouth. Aunt Phyllis said it was like pulling teeth. The doctor told her they'd have to put him in the hospital. Grandpa was entirely too weak to resist.

They gave him a semi-private room. There was another old man in the next bed who'd formed a good relationship with Grandpa. He told us, "Edgar tol' me he wus ti'ed' and wus goin' to lay down and res' a spell, wait on Lula to make his med'cine." He stumbled over to his bed, curled up into a ball, and just laid down and died. That was it. There was never an exact time of death; he died silently and comfortably. If he experienced any pain, no one knew of it.

It was the worst kind of helplessness I'd ever felt. There I was, trapped by the weather at the ends of the earth when I desperately needed to be with Grandma. The Air Force and Red Cross did everything within their power to get me off that rock but there was nothing we could do until the weather cooperated. When the wind finally quelled and the ice thawed, I was able to make my way back down to Anchorage. I still had over two thousand miles to go until I'd be in Birmingham. It was almost two weeks after I got the call before I finally made it back.

Everyone was gathered at Aunt Phyllis' house. Aunts and uncles and grandchildren were coming and going the whole time. Grandma was so glad to see me; we fell into an endless hug. Then I went to Grandpa's grave. It did me a world of good to see it. He was buried in the backyard of his beloved Zion Hill church, next to six of his sisters and brothers. I knew he was at peace. He was resting in his proper place.

When I got back to Aunt Phyllis' house, I went to be with Grandma in her little room. I told her how Grandpa's resting place seemed right to me. She smiled, then silence. She was solemn the whole time I was there. I sat with her and watched as she stared off into space. There was something about just being there, and the silence between us, that was soothing. It was like we were together in the same place in our minds, reflecting and appreciating a thousand precious memories of Grandpa.

She broke her silence and spoke as though he hadn't died at all. I knew that deep inside Grandma's heart, he was alive and well.

That night, from Aunt Phyllis' guest bedroom, I could hear her talking to Grandpa as if he was right there next to her. It was a little spooky, but it brought warmth to my heart knowing that Grandma was okay and feeling Grandpa right by her side as always.

I didn't ask Aunt Phyllis about my quilt and if anyone had found it. It was a time for me to be with Grandma. There was an air of spiritual beauty the whole time. When we parted, we held hands and didn't want to let go.

I spent the next three years in Germany. During that time, I was able to go back to the United States once to see Grandma. By that time, her mind had deteriorated. The usually sharp, on-point Grandma, was long gone. She talked to Grandpa more often than when he first passed away. I would sit and listen and had I not known for a fact that Grandpa was deceased, I'd think he was right there in the other room. Even though Grandma's faculties were deteriorating, she didn't lose sight of who I was. As soon as I entered her room, those gray eyes lit up like a Christmas tree. Her mouth trembled as she tried to ease out my name from her lips.

I gently caressed those old shaking hands that were scarred with the wear and tear from all the quilts she made in her lifetime. Sometimes she'd deviate from talking about or directly to Grandpa, and begin telling the story of Ella. Then out of nowhere, she'd start talking to me like *I* was Ella. I never told her any different. I just listened to the same stories that she'd conveyed to me a million times as a child. I wondered whether she wanted to solidify these tales to make sure I'd never forget them.

After my discharge from the Air Force, I moved to the outskirts of Atlanta, Georgia so I could be closer to Grandma. Birmingham was only a quick ninety-nine miles down Interstate 20. It was heart-wrenching watching Grandma become increasingly immobile.

It had gotten to the point where she could no longer take care of her physical needs like bathing and eating. Aunt Phyllis took impeccable care of her, waiting on her hand and foot. I'd talk to her for a while, but when the tears began welling up, I'd step out right away to regain my composure. I thought it might confuse or upset her to see me crying.

Before I left to go back home to Atlanta, as Grandma lay there in her bed, I kissed her on the forehead and said, "Goodbye Miss Lula." She began moving her lips but her words came out in a whisper. I leaned down and put my ear next to her mouth. She repeated her favorite words to me: "I love your heart and your liv'r, too." I whispered back in her ear, "I love you, too, Grandma." As I left the room, her eyes fixated on my every move. The light in them had diminished, but she looked peaceful.

About a week later, I had a vision. I dreamt I was waiting impatiently for the four o'clock flowers to open at their appointed time. Five o'clock came and went and they never opened; neither did they open at six o'clock. I stood there forever waiting for the buds to open. My tears began to flow. Then the sun came out, and there was Grandma, standing before me as I shielded my face from the sun. She smiled as she brushed the tears from my face. She grabbed my hand and guided me to an old wooden stump that protruded from the ground. She took the comb from her apron pocket and began gently combing my hair, humming my favorite tune. An immense feeling of peace washed over me and led me gently out of my dream, as if by the hand.

I longed to reenter my dream world so I'd be submerged in that feeling again. But the phone rang. It was Aunt Phyllis calling to tell me Grandma had passed away during the night. It was odd; instead of crying, I felt as soothed as I did inside that dream. I knew Grandma was at peace. She had surfaced in my dream world to let me know that she'd never be far from me. It was her way of telling me that whenever I felt lonely and sad, I should think about our days together.

I packed my bags and headed back to Aunt Phyllis' house in Birmingham. It seemed like only yesterday I was in the same spot grieving for Grandpa. Grandpa and Grandma were together again, forever in life and in death. Aunt Phyllis and I embraced for a long, sad time. I went and sat in Grandma's little room, the one she'd occupied for the past twelve years. Her scent filled the air and permeated all of my senses. It became part of me, like my own breath. I was taken back to the old times in that country air and country surroundings where I found my bloodline for the very first time. I sat and rocked in the same rocking chair that Grandpa Edgar sat perched in, all those years ago. It had miraculously survived the fire.

I thought about Miss Sugar and Aunt Honey Bee and Aunt Bessie, who had all long since passed. I recalled those nights sitting with Grandma and Grandpa on the screened-in front porch, listening to the insects as the rest of the world went by. I must have drifted into a memory-filled sleep. The room became chilly. I could feel the draft enter into my dream world. I felt like I did long ago as a child in the country when I just couldn't get warm. Suddenly, a thick layer of warmth descended upon me, taking the chill away. It woke me up from my deep slumber.

I opened my eyes and couldn't believe what I saw. It was *my* quilt, lying right there on top of me like it had floated down from the sky. How was that possible? Was I dreaming that I was awake? It had the same stitching, the same stains embedded into the fibers of each piece, and the same beautiful colors that were imbued with the magic of Grandma Lula's hands and heart.

I was utterly mystified. Tears poured out of my eyes as I gathered that quilt so close to me, I could feel the pulse of every life, every soul woven into those small pieces of cloth that were stitched together to become whole again. Did it fall from the sky? Was it delivered by Grandma's spirit? I wept like a child whose heart was broken. Only this time, those tears were of a woman whose heart was mended.

I looked up and saw my mother standing in the doorway of the room. I thought it was an apparition. She said, "This is your quilt and Grandma wanted you to have it." She explained that all these years she'd kept it in her linen closet and felt now would be the time to return it to me, where it belonged. It took a long time for my emotions to calm down. I went for a walk that night, cradling my quilt as if it were my own child. I returned to the house and joined Aunt Phyllis and my mother in Grandma's little room. We sat there talking about the life and times of Edgar and Lula Horn until daybreak.

Aunt Phyllis told the story about Grandma leaving home for months. She traveled over one hundred miles away in Mississippi where she worked as a maid, servant and primary caretaker for Doc Rogers and his family of four. She nursed, raised, cooked and cleaned house for Doc Rogers and his family from the time their girls were born until they became teenagers. "I'd only see Mama as she was turning her back to leave for another month or so." Aunt Phyllis spoke with such sadness in her voice.

I realized that completely crushed my mother because after her older sister Sarah ran away, she was left to raise her younger sister,

Phyllis, and act as caretaker for my grandfather who always suffered from poor health. Pictures of Doc Rogers' children hung from the mantle of her mother's home in Alabama with pride, and the clothes from Doc Rogers' children were passed on to my mother and her sister. Mother mentioned how it was all about Doc Rogers' children and not much about them during those days.

I was sure those pictures were constant reminders to Mother and solidified the notion that she was only an after-thought in the eyes of Grandma Lula. With each passing year, as another picture of the Rogers' children filled the mantle, a harboring bitterness and contempt built up inside Mother. Even though she appeared to be emotionally and mentally stronger than she actually was, you could detect the pain through the "it didn't bother me" persona.

This was the first time I'd ever heard my mother or Aunt Phyllis openly discuss those years when Grandma worked in Mississippi. Somehow, with Grandma's passing, they were able to speak about it, but not in any great detail. My mother and Aunt Phyllis were young when Grandma went off to work for Doc Rogers. They suffered immeasurably from not having their mother around. It was maternal hemorrhage due to all the siblings being deprived of their mother at such tender ages. Those were difficult times and they missed her terribly. They had to be raised by their sister Sarah, who was only a child herself.

They revealed how they'd cry themselves to sleep at night due to Grandma's absence. This was a double-edged sword because Grandma had to work out of necessity. Grandpa was disabled and couldn't earn a living, so the burden fell on Grandma. Because of her hard work and dedication, she was able to send my mother and Aunt Phyllis to College. Aunt Phyllis earned her Master's Degree in Education.

When Grandma no longer worked for Doc Rogers, she spent long days farming her own land in order to provide for the family. After I returned to Detroit, four or five grandchildren came after me who

Grandma partially raised. Even though it was a struggle for them not having Grandma around, they understood the hard work she endured in order for them to blossom into the women that Grandma hoped they would be.

There was no doubt both those sisters loved Lula Horn with all their hearts. Through a stream of tears, Aunt Phyllis spoke: "Mama was our guiding light." She and Mother held hands as they reflected back on Grandma Lula. Mother turned and looked at me. Softly, almost under her breath like a curse, she said, "You were the one who got to soak up all Mama's love for all those years. We never got much, and there you were, just wallowing in it."

The words nearly knocked me over. The understanding sliced through me like a blade. That was the origin of Mother's anger and hostility. For every strike and lash of the extension cord that she levied against me, she was striking back at her mother for not being there. I was the one that had taken Grandma's love. A deep sorrow came over me, sorrow for the both of us. With that revelation, something opened up between Mother and me that day. I think I forgave her.

The next day at the church, I sat in the back while hundreds of people who loved Grandma filed up to the beautiful blue coffin she rested in to say their goodbyes. I knew Grandma was probably fretting. She didn't like being the center of attention. She was always the one caring for others in their times of need. Whether it was tending to the grieving, cooking for everyone, nursing other people's children, or making beautiful quilts, Grandma Lula was an angel. Her kindness, her wisdom, her warmth and enduring strength manifested itself in the way she lived her life. She was my guide and my teacher. It was from her that I learned to face life and to move forward against all odds. She taught me to endure hardship and be strong.

As the last person trailed up to the front of the church to say goodbye, I gathered myself. It was time for me to come face to face with my grandmother Lula - my friend and my rock- one last time. Not to say goodbye, but to say I love you and thank you for preparing me. I whispered in her ear, "I love your heart and your liver too," then sang the lines of one of her favorite songs:

When I go the last mile of the way
I will pause at the breaking of the day
Remember you said that you would be waiting for me above
Where the four o'clock flowers and the white sandy road meet

I will always love you, Miss Lula.

THE END